D1348057

ALICE'S COOK BOOK

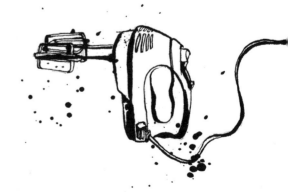

Quadrille
PUBLISHING

Leabharlanna Átha Cliath Theas

★

alice's
COOK
BOOK

ALICE HART

Photography by Emma Lee
Illustrations by Ruth Jackson

For my mum, Jasmine

EDITORIAL DIRECTOR Anne Furniss
CREATIVE DIRECTOR Helen Lewis
PROJECT EDITOR Lucy Bannell
DESIGNER Claire Peters
PHOTOGRAPHER Emma Lee
ILLUSTRATOR Ruth Jackson
STYLIST Tabitha Hawkins
PRODUCTION DIRECTOR Vincent Smith
PRODUCTION CONTROLLER Ruth Deary

First published in 2010 by
Quadrille Publishing Limited
Alhambra House
27-31 Charing Cross Road
London WC2H 0LS
www.quadrille.co.uk

Reprinted in 2010
10 9 8 7 6 5 4 3 2

Text © 2010 Alice Hart
Photographs © 2010 Emma Lee
Design and layout © 2010
Quadrille Publishing Limited

The rights of the author have been asserted. All rights reserved.
No part of this book may be reproduced, stored in a retrieval
system or transmitted in any form or by any means, electronic,
electrostatic, magnetic tape, mechanical, photocopying,
recording or otherwise, without the prior permission in writing
of the publisher.

Cataloguing in Publication Data: a catalogue record for this
book is available from the British Library.

ISBN 978 184400 888 9

Printed in China

The Penguin Book
of English Verse

INTRODUCED AND EDITED BY
JOHN HAYWARD

6/-

It is the feasts enjoyed with friends and family that are always the most fondly remembered. Food eaten at leisure, and in celebration, is the backbone of my cooking and it's become second nature to prepare it without fuss. That's what I want to pass on to you; my strategies for spending time in the kitchen intelligently and enjoyably so that you can feed any number as serenely as possible, because I understand what it's like to have precious little free time.

I'm not really a ready-made food or quick-fix kind of girl; never have been. Please don't see that as a snobbish statement... like you, I have a busy life to lead and am far from a Stepford type. Admittedly, cooking is a priority and a joy for me but I'd rather spend a few minutes making a marinade or cake a day or two before the main event to free up time later. From Sunday lunches to drinks parties to camping trips, some preparation time snatched here and there saves getting flustered on the day. The very idea of chopping madly at the last minute, as the doorbell rings, fills me with horror. I love having friends over, feeding them, cooking for them... why would I want to make it a torture? When lunch is pretty much in the bag, life is more relaxed (and we can all go outside and enjoy the sunshine). This advance prepping is my way of picking a path through life's vicissitudes, with sanity somewhat intact and delectable food on the table.

Deciding what to cook, for any number, can take practice. Each menu in this book has been carefully thought through to make it as seamless as possible and a couple of the more involved meals even contain a time plan to help with the logistics. Oven temperatures have been synched wherever they can be, and last-minute preparation kept to a minimum. Of course, you don't have to cook an entire menu; the individual recipes will stand proudly alone.

While I hesitate to quote dictatorial rules, there are a few that apply to food, to be broken as you wish. Try to introduce contrasts: rich with light; bite with soft; fried with steamed. And, in general, keep to one country or area to avoid muddying flavours; a Thai curry is best with simply steamed rice, rather than a Persian pilaf.

There are lines to be drawn, I feel, when writing and following recipes. Certain detail is, of course, good and necessary - tin size, cooking time and the like - but too much can be obtrusive and quashes natural instinct. My intent is to encourage you to enjoy cooking well and to nurture the appreciation of food it brings. How you get there in your own kitchen will be affected by so many factors; I'm merely here to guide, without smothering or bombarding. So beyond the realms

Clondalkin Library
Monastery Road
Clondalkin
Dublin 22
Ph: 4593315

of exacting baking measurements (use scales) and oven temperatures (get an oven thermometer), do what feels right. Add more chilli if you crave bite; use maple syrup in place of honey. These are your recipes now.

I see a healthy dose of pride and enthusiasm for cooking, particularly among my contempories. Because we seem bashful about our culinary credentials in Britain, sparks from other, more exotic, cuisines are happily embraced. And with today's horizons broader than ever, our kitchens sing with every new spice and herb.

Each place I visit has had an impact on my food, be it an animated corner of Asia or a Devon tea house that restores one's faith in scones. You'll find a few Vietnamese, Thai, Italian, Moroccan and Indian-influenced recipes peppered throughout this book, because those cuisines inspire me. But the emphasis lies with following the British seasons, sticking with our own best ingredients.

These menus are seasonal, but can be easily adapted to use the produce that is best in the month during which you are cooking. Sub in like for like - leaf for leaf or root for root - and problems will be unlikely. Seaonal eating is important not merely because of the superior taste of produce at its peak, but because it is an economical way to dine; a way to avoid compromise by buying when gluts force prices down, meaning I can just about afford those chubby vanilla pods, say, or that spry olive oil, to set them off.

This isn't principally a book of everyday food, though you will find many simple ideas for lunch and supper, but I hope you'll invent reasons to celebrate and to cook from it often. That's the point: the recipes are meant to make dinners, parties or expeditions to the North Pole both more enjoyable and more attainable. Corny it may be, but love, laughter and eating well are bound together and that should always be so.

It is more fun to talk with someone who doesn't use long, difficult words but rather short, easy words like "What about lunch?"

WINNIE THE POOH
FROM THE HOUSE AT POOH CORNER BY A A MILNE

★

BREAKFAST
AND BRUNCH

FROM THE HASTILY SCOFFED BUTTIE TO THE LEISURELY BRUNCH, STRETCHING LUNCHWARDS, THE FIRST FUEL OF THE DAY HAS MORE IMPORTANCE THAN MOST OF US ASCRIBE TO IT. BE THAT AS IT MAY, IN MY EXPERIENCE A LOVINGLY PREPARED BREAKFAST USUALLY COMES SECOND BEST TO SLEEPING, RUNNING ABOUT OR WHATEVER ELSE YOU CHOOSE TO DO WITH YOUR EARLY MORNINGS SO, IF YOU CAN BEAR IT, DOING A BIT OF EASY PREP THE NIGHT BEFORE IS THE KEY TO FEEDING LARGER NUMBERS.

EASY, PORTABLE BREAKFAST
FOR A CROWD OF EIGHT

Apple and Almond Bircher

Boursin Omelette Baguettes

Honey's Raspberry Turnovers

Destined for autumn, this is a weekend spread to
lay out on the table and leave there when you've got
a full house. Sometimes, getting everybody up at the
same time, let alone sitting around a table,
is too much to ask. None of these recipes will mind
waiting around until an owner scoops them up.
They'll need lots of hot coffee, tea or juice to go
with them. For proper stragglers, much of breakfast
is portable; perfect for eating on the hoof
(or spreading crumbs around the car) if you've
got somewhere to be.

APPLE AND ALMOND BIRCHER

HANDS-ON TIME: 15 MINUTES

FOR THE BIRCHER
300g rolled oats
350ml English cloudy
  apple juice
150ml milk or water
150g whole almonds,
  roughly chopped,
  or flaked almonds
3 British eating apples

TO SERVE
milk
thick, natural yogurt
4 tbsp mixed seeds
  (sunflower, sesame,
  pumpkin)
seasonal berries or extra
  chopped apple
mild runny honey

Bircher muesli is an embarrassingly easy recipe that still manages to impress everyone. It is always especially popular with healthy-living types. Vary the components as you like, but keep the basic oat-to-liquid ratio the same. A bowl of the soaked oats and fruit juice will keep in the refrigerator for several days, ready to be further customised with extra fruit, nuts, seeds, yogurt and milk.

The night before, or at least a couple of hours before you want to eat, mix the oats, apple juice and milk or water with half the almonds in a large bowl. Cover with a plate and refrigerate.

When you're ready for breakfast, coarsely grate the apples, avoiding the cores, and fold into the oat mixture. Let everyone construct their own bowlfuls of muesli, adding milk and/or yogurt, a spoonful of the remaining almonds, seeds, berries, apple or honey to sweeten.

HONEY'S RASPBERRY TURNOVERS

HANDS-ON TIME: 15 MINUTES

flour, to dust
500g all-butter puff pastry
500g fresh raspberries
about 125g vanilla sugar
  or caster sugar
1 free-range egg yolk,
  mixed with 1 tbsp milk

Honey, my baker-extraordinaire, puff-pastry-making grandmother, has been a dab hand with a turnover for as long as I can remember, churning out batches of apple, apricot or raspberry from a handsome blue Aga. Make sure you use all-butter puff pastry; it tastes better and it has a much more wholesome ingredients list than the dubious vegetable fat types.

On a lightly floured surface, roll out the pastry to form a ½cm thick rectangle. Use a sharp knife to trim the raggedy edges straight, then cut into eight even squares. They should each be about 15x15cm.

Place a pile of raspberries in each square, slightly off-centre, and add a heaped teaspoon of sugar. With a pastry brush, paint a little water around the edge and bring one corner over to meet its diagonal opposite. Press the edges together firmly to seal, using the tines of a fork if you like. Repeat to make eight pastries, spacing them out on a baking tray. At this stage, the turnovers may be chilled for up to two days.

Preheat the oven to 200°C/fan 190°C/400°F/gas mark 6. Brush the pastry surfaces with the egg wash (yolk and milk mixture) and sprinkle with a little more sugar. Cut a small vent in the top of each to let the steam out and bake for about 20 minutes, until exuberantly plump and golden. Cool on a wire rack and serve warm.

BOURSIN OMELETTE BAGUETTES won't mind sitting about for a bit at room temperature, ready to be re-warmed in a low oven when any stragglers find their way to the kitchen. Make two at a time. Warm a couple of lengths of very fresh French bread in the oven. Meanwhile, beat three or four free-range eggs lightly in a bowl. Add just a little seasoning and a couple of tablespoons of coarsely crumbled Boursin (garlic and herb) soft cheese. Melt a knob of butter in a frying pan and, when foaming, tip in your eggs, shaking the pan as they hit the hot butter. As the egg cooks, draw it in from the edges with a spoon or spatula and tilt the pan to allow the raw egg to run into the space. When almost cooked, but still a little runny, split the warmed bread and spread with butter and more Boursin. Fold the omelette over and tip out of the pan. Cut in half and stuff into a baguette. Add a few halved cherry tomatoes, and/or a handful of peppery rocket leaves, if you like.

NEW YEAR BRUNCH FOR EIGHT

Crisp, Maple-Sugared Bacon with
Oven Hash Browns and Poached Eggs

Proper Baked Beans

Orchard Pastries

Mocha Affogatos

Pomegranate Fizz

Unless you like cooking on a snatched few hours of
sleep, this is probably a menu for a civilised New
Year, or at least for a late brunch. That's not to
say it's difficult; there are a few tricks tucked in
the methods to make life easier. Do a head-count
for any non-meat eaters in advance and make the
veggie version of the beans (and don't offer any
bacon) to keep everyone happy.

CRISP, MAPLE-SUGARED BACON WITH OVEN HASH BROWNS AND POACHED EGGS

HANDS-ON TIME: 15 MINUTES

FOR THE HASH BROWNS
2 large baking potatoes
2 large sweet potatoes
1 small onion, finely sliced
small bunch of chives,
  snipped
6 tbsp olive oil

FOR THE BACON
16 rashers free-range
  streaky bacon
3 tbsp maple syrup
a pinch of cayenne pepper

TO SERVE
8 very fresh, free-range
  eggs
Easy Tomato, Pepper and
  Chilli Jam (see page 32)

Do keep an eye on the bacon, but, as someone who burns toast, bacon and nuts with frustrating regularity, gentle cooking rather than grilling is far less risky. There are lots of tricks for poaching eggs, but I find vinegar in the water produces vinegary egg whites, while whirling vortexes in the pan aren't much use when you're cooking eight eggs. The very best advice is to use the freshest eggs you can find. And lastly, oven hash browns mean no more uncooked potato centres and less time peering into a frying pan.

Preheat the oven to 180°C/fan 170°C/350°F/gas mark 4. Peel the potatoes and grate coarsely. Pile into a clean tea towel with the onion, twist into a cracker shape and wring hard to squeeze out excess water. Shake into a bowl and add the chives, half the oil and plenty of seasoning. Generously oil two 12-hole bun tins and flatten a tight-packed ball of potato into each (or cook on a large baking tray, spacing out well). Bake on the middle shelf for 40 minutes, until golden and toasted at the edges. Keep an eye on them, as stray strands like to singe. Combine the bacon, syrup and cayenne in a bowl, then lay on an oiled baking tray. Cook on the shelf above the hash browns for 25–30 minutes, turning halfway, until darkly golden and crisp.

About 10 minutes before the hash browns are done, fill a large, deep-sided frying pan with water and bring up to simmering point. The water should be barely bubbling. Crack an egg into a teacup and, very carefully, slide it into the water. Repeat with the remaining eggs. Cook for three minutes until the whites are just set, then fish out with a slotted spoon and lay on a plate lined with kitchen towel.

Serve the eggs, hash browns and bacon with a dollop of Easy Tomato, Pepper and Chilli Jam (see page 32). Good old ketchup or HP makes a winning accompaniment, too.

PROPER BAKED BEANS

HANDS-ON TIME: 15 MINUTES

500g dried borlotti beans
2 tbsp treacle or dark
  muscovado sugar
1 heaped tsp English
  mustard powder
1 onion, chopped
400g can chopped
  tomatoes
1 rosemary sprig
1 small, smoked ham hock
  (optional)

A slightly cheaty title because these beans aren't even half-baked; they're cooked on the hob to free up the oven space. Do bake them at a low temperature if you like (at 160°C/ fan 150°C/325°F/gas mark 3). Replace the dried beans, at the point when they have been simmered in water for an hour, with drained canned beans to cut down on the cooking time, but it won't be as satisfyingly thrifty. (You'll need four 400g cans of borlotti beans.) The smoked ham hock is rather wonderful, but if you'd rather keep the beans vegetarian, replace it with a few sun-dried tomatoes and 1 tsp smoked paprika. The cooked beans will keep in the refrigerator for at least a week.

Soak the beans for at least eight hours, or overnight, in plenty of cold water. If you forget, or don't have time for such a long soaking, cover them with cold water in a large saucepan, bring to the boil and simmer briskly for a few minutes before setting aside to cool for an hour or two. Either way, drain the beans, cover with fresh water and bring to a rolling boil. Simmer for an hour, until just tender. Drain, but reserve the cooking water.

Mix the cooked beans (or canned beans, if you've read the recipe introduction) with the remaining ingredients in a large saucepan and cover with 500ml of the reserved cooking liquid, or with fresh water if you're using canned beans. Cover, then simmer very gently for an hour or so, until completely tender. If you used it, fish out the ham hock and cut the meat into small pieces, discarding bone, fat and gristle. Return the meat to the beans and season to taste with pepper and a little salt, if needed.

ORCHARD PASTRIES

HANDS-ON TIME: 20 MINUTES

350g all-butter puff pastry or 2 x Quick Flaky Pastry recipe (see page 78)
plain flour, to dust
1 free-range egg
2 tbsp soft light brown sugar
2 tbsp cream cheese
1 tbsp ground almonds
½ tsp ground cinnamon
1 eating apple, quartered, cored and thinly sliced
1 ripe pear, quartered, cored and sliced
a little milk
2 tbsp soft-set apricot jam

Ripe plums, apricots or peaches make lovely stand-ins for these pears and apples during the warmer months. Just use whatever's good and seasonal.

Roll the puff pastry or Quick Flaky Pastry out on a lightly floured surface and cut into eight squares, each about 13x13cm. Preheat the oven to 180°C/fan 170°C/350°F/gas mark 4.

Beat the egg, sugar, cream cheese, almonds and cinnamon together and spoon into the centre of each pastry square.

Top each square with sliced apple or pear, fanning the pieces out slightly. Pinch two diagonal pastry corners together and dab with milk to seal (it should be a square with pointy ends). Brush the pastry surface with a little more milk. Space out on a large baking tray and cook for 15 minutes or so, until the pastry is golden. Cool on the baking tray for five minutes before moving them to a cooling rack. Spread the fruit with a little jam, using the back of a teaspoon, and eat warm or leave to cool.

MOCHA AFFOGATOS

HANDS-ON TIME: 10 MINUTES

8 small scoops best-quality
  chocolate ice cream
250ml hot, freshly brewed
  strong espresso
60g best-quality dark
  chocolate, coarsely grated

Affogatos are traditionally taken later in the day, though I don't see why they shouldn't make a chic appearance at brunch. Give in to the allure of the morning gelato! Use vanilla ice cream if chocolate seems too much, but this mocha version is delicious. There's nowhere for the ingredients to hide, so use the very best quality ice cream, coffee and chocolate you can afford.

Divide the ice cream between eight sturdy small glasses or cups. Top each scoop with a dash of espresso and sprinkle with a little grated chocolate. Serve immediately, with teaspoons, before too much melting occurs.

A decadent **POMEGRANATE FIZZ** should complement all things brunch. Squeeze the juice from one large or two small pomegranates. The easiest way is to halve the fruit and crush/squeeze them into a bowl just as you would a lemon. Strain the juice through a tea strainer into a jug because it's bound to have stray seeds and bit of pith in it. Divide the juice between eight champagne glasses and fill up with chilled champagne, prosecco or dry sparkling white.

BUTTERY APPLE, HONEY AND POLENTA LOAF CAKE

SERVES 8-10
HANDS-ON TIME: 20 MINUTES

FOR THE CAKE
250g unsalted butter,
  softened
200g mild, set British
  honey
3 large free-range eggs
100g ground almonds
150g plain flour, sifted
150g polenta
2 lemons, finely grated zest
  of both, juice of 1
2 British eating apples,
  quartered, cored and
  chopped small
1 tsp baking powder
½ tsp salt

FOR THE GLAZE
60g mild, set British honey
1 lemon, juice only

A simple, rustic cake for a crowd, with a light and lemony syrup to pour over as it cools. My grandparents have kept bees by the South Downs for more than 50 years and, although they can't produce and pot the honey themselves any more, the hives are still in use. The gently flavoured set honey their bees make is perfect for this cake, though any mild honey would work, as would runny honey. I like to use chopped Egremont Russets in the batter, but little Cox's Orange Pippins, or similar, will also be grand.

Line a 1kg or 11x21cm loaf tin with non-stick baking parchment. Preheat the oven to 180°C/fan 170°C/350°F/gas mark 4.

Beat the butter and honey together until light and fluffy. Add the eggs, one at a time, beating well between each addition to make the batter light, then fold in the remaining cake ingredients. Spoon into the tin, level the top with the back of a spoon and bake for an hour, or until well-risen and golden.

Turn out on to a wire rack, right-side up, and pierce several times with a skewer. To make the glaze, gently heat the honey in a small pan and stir in the lemon juice. Allow to cool for a couple of minutes. Place a plate under the cake to catch the run-off and spoon the warm glaze over the cake. Serve warm or cool, as it is, or with natural yogurt and/or apple compote for brunch.

**SPRING BREAKFAST
FOR SIX AT THE WEEKEND
(TO MAKE THE NIGHT BEFORE)**

Maple and Blueberry Sticky Buns

Tropical Fruit Platter with Kaffir Lime

Sunshine Juice

The smell of yeasty, maple-spiked dough baking could sell any house in the land. If you make and knead the dough the night before, you too can have a kitchen as fragrantly delicious as a bakery (and all will marvel at your genius). Make the fruit salad beforehand too, and chill until the morning. The juice only takes a very few minutes on the day.

TROPICAL FRUIT PLATTER
WITH KAFFIR LIME

HANDS-ON TIME: 20 MINUTES

4 tbsp caster sugar

2 small kaffir lime leaves, finely sliced (or the finely grated zest of 1 lime)

2 limes, juice only

2 ripe mangoes

1 ripe pineapple, peeled, cored and chopped into wedges

1 fat wedge from a large watermelon, skin removed and flesh sliced

1 ripe papaya, peeled, halved, deseeded and sliced

12 fresh lychees, peeled and stoned, or a 400g can lychees, drained

It almost goes without saying that the fruit can be varied according to whim or weather; just choose the sweetest and ripest you can find.

Gently heat the sugar with 4 tbsp water until it dissolves. Bring to the boil, then remove from the heat and add the kaffir lime leaves (or lime zest) and lime juice. Set aside.

To prepare the mango, cut the fat cheeks from either side of the flat stone. Score the flesh in a cross-hatch pattern and turn the skin 'inside out' so that the mango flesh looks like cuboid hedgehog spikes. Cut the cubes off, leaving the skin behind.

Arrange all the fruit on a serving plate and spoon the kaffir lime syrup over. Cover and chill for an hour, or up to eight hours, to infuse the fruit with the kaffir lime.

MAPLE AND BLUEBERRY STICKY BUNS

HANDS-ON TIME: 30 MINUTES

FOR THE MAPLE BUTTER
150g unsalted butter,
  softened
100ml maple syrup
150g soft light brown sugar

FOR THE BUNS
340ml milk
60g unsalted butter, plus
  more for the tin
25g fresh yeast,
  or 2 tbsp dried yeast,
  or 1 tbsp fast-action
  dried yeast
60g soft light brown sugar
375g tipo 00 flour, or best-
  quality plain flour, sifted,
  plus more to dust
1 tsp salt
150g dried blueberries
3 tbsp maple syrup

If you want to bake a batch of sweet, sticky buns in the morning, leave the dough to rise in the refrigerator overnight, then shape and bake the next day. This makes 12 buns, but I don't think that will be a major problem...

Start with the maple butter. Beat the butter, syrup and sugar until light, then set aside at room temperature.

For the buns, heat the milk and, just before it boils, add the butter. Set aside until cooled to blood temperature.

Meanwhile, measure 100ml of warm water into a small jug. Stir in the yeast and a large pinch of the sugar. Leave it in a warm place to activate for five minutes or so; the yeast should bubble up to form a lovely frothy top.

Place all the remaining sugar, flour and salt in a large bowl and make a well in the centre. Add the activated yeast and the buttery milk and bring together with your hands to form a dough. Knead for eight to 10 minutes on a floured surface until the dough is silky smooth and elastic, then transfer to an oiled bowl. (The easier option is to use a dough hook attachment on a food mixer to form and knead the dough. If you do let a mixer take the strain, the kneading will only take five minutes.)

Cover the bowl with oiled clingfilm and leave to rise in a warm place for an hour. You can leave it in the refrigerator overnight instead if it's easier, but make sure to bring it to room temperature before proceeding with the recipe.

Preheat the oven to 200°C/fan 190°C/400°F/gas mark 6. Once the dough has risen, knock it back with a satisfying punch, dust with flour and knead it for a minute. Roll and stretch out to form a large rectangle (about 25x40cm). Spread the dough with two-thirds of the maple butter and sprinkle with the dried blueberries. Fold the bottom third up from the longest side and the top third down on to this, as if you were folding a letter to put in an envelope. Now gently roll the dough out to a large rectangle as before and spread with the remaining maple butter. This time, roll up from a long edge to form a log-shape.

Cut the log into 12 even pieces that will look like pinwheels. Butter a 12-hole muffin tin and place a bun, cut side uppermost, in each space. Leave the buns to puff up in a warm place for 10 minutes, drizzle with the 3 tbsp maple syrup and bake for 30 minutes. Carefully remove from the tins while hot, or they'll stick, but allow them to cool a little before eating.

Been overdoing the parties and the sticky buns? A **SUNSHINE JUICE** should begin to sort things out... You'll need a fruit and veg juicer to make this, unless you mix fresh apple, orange and carrot juice in a jug with squeezed-out ginger pulp and ice cubes. For each serving, juice two carrots, one apple, one large orange and half a thumb's-worth of fresh root ginger. Stir and serve the juice as soon as possible to get the best out of the vitamins.

SUMMER BRUNCH FOR 12

Baked Pistachio Granola,
Apricot Compote and Yogurt

■

Sugared Brioche Perdu;
Crushed Strawberries

■

Brunch Frittata; Easy Tomato,
Pepper and Chilli Jam

■

Cheddar Cornbread Muffins

■

Mango Lassi

■

Iced Coffee

Twelve is a lovely number for brunch and chat,
but not such a lovely number to cook complicated,
individual egg orders for... especially when you
might all be able to sit outside, be it around a table
or on picnic blankets. For that reason, and without
sacrificing taste, this is another menu of good-natured
beauties. They are all placid enough to sit about for
a while and won't be much trouble to get together
in the first place. Any minutes you can spare the day
before will put you ahead, come the morning.

MANGO LASSI

HANDS-ON TIME: 15 MINUTES

3 large and ripe, fragrant
  mangoes or 600ml
  Alphonso mango puree
600ml thick, natural
  yogurt
600ml chilled water
3 handfuls of crushed ice
sugar or mild honey, to
  taste (optional)

*On hot days, this cooling Indian drink is incredibly
refreshing. If you'd prefer something salty (and this is
much nicer than it sounds), leave out the mango, sugar or
honey. Replace them with a pinch each of toasted cumin
seeds and salt. You can also add a touch of grated fresh root
ginger to the sweet or salty versions before blending.*

Skin and stone the mangoes, then roughly chop the flesh.

Whiz a third of all the ingredients together in a blender
until smooth, then taste and decide if it's sweet enough
for you. If not, add a little sugar or honey and blend again.
Divide between four glasses. Repeat twice more to fill the
remaining eight glasses.

Making **ICED COFFEE** the night before is
so much easier than brewing up fresh espresso
after fresh espresso to order, and a cold drink
can easily be justified on a summer's day.
You can also make it pretty strong and dilute
with milk or iced water for those of more
delicate constitutions. Measure 2 tbsp coffee
and 100ml of water per person into a large
jug. Stir well and chill in the refrigerator
overnight. The next morning, add another
100ml of chilled water per person, stir again
and strain through a fine sieve. Serve the
chilled coffee over ice, topped up with plenty
of chilled milk and as much sugar as you like.

BAKED PISTACHIO GRANOLA, APRICOT COMPOTE AND YOGURT

HANDS-ON TIME: 25 MINUTES

FOR THE GRANOLA
1 large Bramley apple,
  peeled, cored and
  chopped
225ml maple syrup
600g oats
60g each sesame, pumpkin
  and sunflower seeds
75g shelled, unsalted
  pistachios, roughly
  chopped
2 tbsp walnut, almond or
  mild olive oil
½ tsp ground cinnamon
250g dried apricots,
  snipped into pieces

FOR THE COMPOTE
1 vanilla pod, split
  lengthwise
18 small, ripe apricots,
  halved and stoned
100ml maple syrup

TO SERVE
ice-cold milk and natural
  yogurt

Which genius came up with the idea of eating oat biscuits with milk for breakfast? That's basically what the more sugary, fatty granolas are. At the risk of sounding like a control freak, making your own cereal allows you to tweak the oil and sugar levels, resulting in a vastly superior granola. When it comes to oats, play around and see what you like best. I tend to use 450g whole rolled oats and 150g porridge oats for the robust texture I prefer. Any left over will keep for a few days in an airtight tin. Obviously, it will become worryingly addictive once you know it's to hand.

Start with a quick apple sauce for the granola: gently heat the chopped apple in a saucepan with a splash of water. Cover and simmer very gently for 10 minutes, until the apple breaks down. Stir in 25ml of the syrup and set aside.

Preheat the oven to 160°C/fan 150°C/325°F/gas mark 3. Combine the apple sauce with all the remaining granola ingredients except the apricots and spread out on a large baking sheet lined with non-stick baking parchment. Cook for 25 minutes, stirring at least every 10 to make sure it gilds evenly. Add the apricots and cook for 10–15 minutes more. Do keep an eye on it and reduce the heat if it browns too quickly. Cool the granola on the tray and use right away or store in an airtight container in a cool, dark place for up to three weeks. Refresh by giving it a blast in a hot oven to re-crisp if the oats start to go soft.

While the granola cooks, make the compote. Scrape the seeds from the vanilla pod with the tip of a knife. Heat the apricots, syrup, vanilla pod and seeds in a small pan over gentle heat, until soft. Stir now and then, but remove from the heat before the apricots start to lose their shape (about 10 minutes). Leave to cool, then fish out the vanilla pod and serve the fruit with the cold cereal and milk or yogurt.

EASY TOMATO, PEPPER AND CHILLI JAM

MAKES 3 JARS
HANDS-ON TIME: 15 MINUTES

2 fat, peeled garlic cloves
3 long red chillies
15g fresh root ginger, peeled
300g ripe tomatoes
2 red peppers, deseeded
150g demerara sugar
½ tsp salt, or 1 tbsp fish sauce
4 tbsp rice vinegar

A sweet-hot jam to make any savoury breakfast great; this is particularly wonderful with herby, baked ricotta. Make it in late summer, when tomatoes, sweet peppers and chillies are at their best.

Whizz the garlic, chillies and fresh root ginger in a mini food processor until finely chopped.

Chop the tomatoes roughly and the peppers a little more finely. Put everything in a large saucepan with the demerara, salt or fish sauce and vinegar.

Bring to the boil and simmer for about half an hour, stirring often, until reduced and viscous. Pot up in warm, sterilised jars (see page 89), screw on the lids tightly and turn upside down to cool. Keep in the refrigerator and use within four months.

BRUNCH FRITTATA WITH EASY TOMATO, PEPPER AND CHILLI JAM

HANDS-ON TIME: 25 MINUTES

8 free-range chipolatas
2 red peppers, deseeded
   and thickly sliced
olive oil
1 large bunch spring
   onions, trimmed
   and sliced
150g mushrooms, sliced
1 garlic clove, finely
   chopped
small handful coriander or
   parsley leaves, chopped
4 tsp Easy Tomato, Pepper
   and Chilli Jam, (see page
   32) (or bought tomato
   chutney or chilli jam)
6 tsp Greek yogurt or
   crème fraîche
6 large, free-range eggs,
   lightly beaten

Don't feel constrained by the brunch name-checking of the title: breakfast, supper or lunch are all eminently suitable occasions for a hearty frittata.

Preheat the grill to medium and toss the sausages and peppers with a little olive oil. Grill on a baking tray for about 10 minutes, turning frequently. Any blackening on the peppers is nothing to worry about. Set aside to cool, then chop the sausages into large chunks.

In a very large frying pan (about 30cm diameter), fry the spring onions in a little oil for two minutes. Add the mushrooms and garlic and sauté for a further five to seven minutes. Stir in the herbs, peppers and sausages, distributing everything evenly. Season well and spoon dollops of the Chilli Jam and yogurt about the pan. Pour in the eggs, cook over a medium-low heat for 10 minutes, then grill for another five to 10 minutes, until just set. Allow to rest for 10 minutes before cutting into wedges and serving with extra Chilli Jam and warm Cheddar Cornbread Muffins (see page 34).

CHEDDAR CORNBREAD MUFFINS

HANDS-ON TIME: 20 MINUTES

2 tbsp olive oil, plus more
  for the tin
160g mature Cheddar
  cheese
300g fine cornmeal
  or polenta
150g plain flour, sifted
1 tsp baking powder
½ tsp bicarbonate of soda
½ tsp salt
2 free-range eggs
280ml pot buttermilk
175ml milk
2 mild red chillies,
  deseeded and chopped
2 tbsp chopped coriander

Tender little bundles to break open and eat while warm and melty. Truly lovely with Frittata (see page 33) and Easy Tomato, Pepper and Chilli Jam (see page 32).

Preheat the oven to 190°C/fan 180°C/375°F/gas mark 5. Oil a non-stick 12-hole muffin tin. Coarsely grate 100g of the Cheddar and cut the remainder into 12 cubes.

Combine all the dry ingredients in a mixing bowl and add the eggs, buttermilk, milk, oil, grated cheese, chilli and coriander. Divide between the holes of the mould and push a cheese cube into the centre of each. Bake for about 20 minutes. When they are risen and smelling delicious, remove from the oven and cool slightly on wire racks. These are best eaten warm.

SUGARED BRIOCHE PERDU; CRUSHED STRAWBERRIES

HANDS-ON TIME: 15 MINUTES

FOR THE BRIOCHE PERDU
60g unsalted butter,
   melted, plus more for
   the dish
12 slices brioche
   (about 400g)
5 free-range eggs,
   lightly beaten
400ml milk
300g crème fraîche
2 tsp vanilla extract
good grating of nutmeg
200g demerara sugar

FOR THE STRAWBERRIES
800g (2 large punnets)
   British strawberries,
   hulled, halved if large
100g caster sugar
3 tbsp good balsamic
   vinegar

Sliced brioche, quite purposely 'lost' in soothing custard under a sweetly crunchy top, is a little gem. The Italians know a thing or two about the luscious strawberries of which we're so proud in Britain. Gentle crushing and a smattering of vinegar or citrus juice brighten them up no end. Make the brioche concoction up to the point of cooking the day before, then refrigerate overnight. Let the dish sit at room temperature for 20 minutes before cooking, to take off the chill.

Generously butter some kind of gratin dish - a large one - and lay in the slices of brioche, overlapping. Make sure there is an odd corner poking out to crisp up in the oven.

Whisk the eggs, milk, crème fraîche, vanilla, nutmeg and 150g of the sugar together. Slowly pour over the brioche, giving the liquid in the bowl the odd stir to distribute the sugar evenly as you pour.

When ready to cook, preheat the oven to 180°C/fan 170°C/350°F/gas mark 4. Take the brioche perdu out of the refrigerator and leave it on the side while the oven heats up. Sprinkle the top with the remaining sugar, drizzle with the melted butter and bake for about 40 minutes, until proudly puffed and golden.

Meanwhile, tip the strawberries into a bowl, add the sugar and vinegar and crush gently with a fork. Leave to macerate at room temperature for half an hour or so.

Let the cooked brioche settle for five minutes before plating up generous squares with a good spoonful of crushed strawberries.

Could anyone refuse a freshly made **SCOTCH PANCAKE** (or drop scone, for that matter)? To make enough for two very hungry people or three not-quite-so-hungry ones, mix 100g self-raising flour, 2 tbsp caster sugar and a pinch of salt in a bowl. Make a well in the middle, break in a free-range egg and slowly pour in 125ml milk as you stir from the inside out with a fork. When all is smooth and the consistency of double cream, heat a heavy, flat griddle or large frying pan over medium heat. Butter it very lightly and drop on spoonfuls of batter to make several roundish pancakes. When the bubbles that rise to the surface of each begin to burst, flip the pancakes over (the cooked surface should be golden) and cook for a further minute. Keep the pancakes on a warm plate, covered with a tea towel, while you cook the rest. Serve, in stacks of joy, with butter and strawberry jam.

Setting up a **BLOODY MARY** station is a cunning way to side-step making the drinks. Fill a couple of large bowls with ice cubes; sit a large jug of chilled tomato juice in one and a smaller jug of chilled vodka in the other. Bottles of Worcestershire and Tabasco sauces, cracked black pepper, celery salt, lots of wedged lemons and limes and an army of tumblers, each containing a celery stick for stirring, should complete the line-up and be enough for most variations. Keep extra ice on hand.

Good bread, warmed through or toasted and eaten with warm, **BAKED RICOTTA**, sliced avocado and the ripest tomato makes a stunning brunch dish. To bake the ricotta for four, mix 250g of the fresh cheese with a free-range egg, a chopped red chilli and soft herbs, such as coriander, parsley or basil. Season well and spoon into a small, oiled dish. Bake at 180°C/fan 170°C/350°F/gas mark 4 for about 25 minutes.

You can bend the rules with brunch, moving things up a notch from typical breakfast fare. To make a luscious, sweet and salty **STICKY RICE WITH MANGO** for six, gently steam 300g Thai sticky or glutinous rice for about 30 minutes in a steamer lined with muslin. Combine 560ml canned coconut milk in a separate saucepan with 5 tbsp granulated sugar and 1¼ tsp salt, stirring over a gentle heat until the sugar has dissolved. Stir the warm sticky rice into the coconut mixture and serve spoonfuls with slices of vibrant, ripe mango. Pour a little extra coconut cream over the top.

Proper **PORRIDGE** is a world away from the vile instant stuff. As the daughter of a Scotsman, I was brought up to prefer my frugal porridge made with water and salt, having first soaked the oats overnight, but admittedly that won't be to everybody's taste. If you'd rather be more indulgent, use proper steel-cut oats or rolled oats, add the tiniest pinch of salt and simmer slowly and gently in milk, or milk and water, stirring often, until done to your liking. Serve with fresh berries - or whatever fruit's in season - Jersey cream and perhaps some golden syrup, jam or toffee-like brown sugar on the side.

America knows a thing or two about baking and brunch. **POPOVERS**, though taller and more elegant, have much in common with the Yorkshire pudding, with a nod to the muffin. Plain or sweetened vanilla versions make neat little carriers for fruit preserves and unsalted butter, but I prefer my popovers savoury. Preheat the oven to 200°C/fan 190°C/400°F/gas mark 6 and butter and flour a six-hole muffin tin, the sort for large muffins. Mix 110g plain flour, ½ tsp salt and 3 tbsp finely grated parmesan. Whisk together a small handful of shredded basil, two large free-range eggs and 240ml milk and add to the dry ingredients, mixing until smooth. Divide between the muffin holes and dust more grated cheese over the top. Bake for 10 minutes, then reduce the heat to 180°C/fan 170°C/350°F/gas mark 4 and cook for 15–20 minutes, until golden and proudly puffed. Make a slit in the side of each to let the steam escape and serve warm. They can be reheated as needed and freeze well, too.

Wash a couple of large handfuls of spinach and briefly wilt over medium heat in the water that still clings to the leaves. Squeeze out any excess water with your hands and combine with a generous handful of grated Wensleydale cheese, a chopped tomato, two beaten free-range eggs and a few sliced spring onions. Season well. Place a frying pan over medium heat, drizzle with olive oil and put in a soft flour tortilla. Spread with half the spinach mixture and top with a second tortilla, pressing down firmly with a fish slice or spatula, or with your hand. Reduce the heat and cook for a few minutes, then flip and cook for a couple of minutes more. Repeat with the remaining filling and more tortillas to make another **QUESADILLA**. Slice them into generous wedges and serve while still warm.

The night before, freeze two bananas in their skins. In the morning, remove and discard the skins and chop the bananas into the jug of a blender with two very ripe chopped figs, 1 tbsp or so of honey, the scraped-out seeds from a vanilla pod, 50ml chilled milk and about 250ml natural yogurt. Puree until the mixture is very smooth and add more chilled milk if it's a bit thick for your liking. Serve the **FROZEN BANANA SMOOTHIE** as soon as possible, in tall glasses.

★

PICNICS, CAMPER
VANS AND HAPPY
CAMPING

HOLIDAYS AND WEEKENDS ARE SUPPOSED
TO BE JUST THAT. DON'T MAKE THINGS
TOO DIFFICULT FOR YOURSELF WITH
OVER-AMBITIOUS COOKING WHEN
THERE'S A GREAT OUTDOORS TO
EXPLORE. RECIPES TO COOK OUTSIDE
OR IN MAKESHIFT KITCHENS HAVE TO
BE STRIPPED DOWN AND SIMPLIFIED AS
MUCH AS THEY'LL ALLOW. MAKE CAKES
AND THE LIKE IN ADVANCE AND TAKE
THEM WITH YOU, STEERING AWAY FROM
ANYTHING WITH DELICATE ICING THAT
COULD GET SPOILED OR CRUSHED.
PACKAGES OF SALT, PEPPER, OIL (IF YOU'LL
BE COOKING) AND THE BARE MINIMUM
OF STORE CUPBOARD INGREDIENTS ARE
ALL YOU'LL NEED. TAKE A COOL BOX
AND ICE BLOCKS IF YOU'RE A SERIOUS
CAMPER. HOPEFULLY, THERE'LL BE A FEW
FORAGING OPPORTUNITIES - FISH AND
FUNGI AND THE LIKE - ALONG THE WAY.

NOW, A LITTLE GENTLE NAGGING.
OPEN-AIR FIRES CAN BE CONTENTIOUS
AND DANGEROUS, SO MAKE SURE YOU
HAVE PERMISSION TO BUILD A CAMP
FIRE OR BARBECUE. USE A SHELTERED
BEACH WHERE FIRES ARE PERMITTED,
OR A CLEARING IN A PRIVATE WOOD
AFTER YOU'VE GOT PERMISSION FROM
THE OWNER. BE SENSIBLE; YOU CAN'T
JUST STRIKE UP THE MATCHES IN A PARK,
AND NOBODY WANTS AN ANGRY FARMER
TRAMPING ACROSS THEIR JOLLY CAMP
FIRE SCENE. LEAVE EVERYTHING AS YOU
FOUND IT: MAKE SURE THE EMBERS ARE
DEAD, RE-COVER THE AREA WITH EARTH
OR SAND AND REMOVE EVERY SCRAP OF
RUBBISH. YOU SHOULD BE ABLE TO TURN
AROUND AND WONDER WHERE THE FIRE
WAS. ALTERNATIVELY, YOU COULD BEG,
BORROW OR BUY A CAMPER VAN, THE
ULTIMATE IN MOBILE KITCHENS.

EARLY AUTUMN WALK ON THE DOWNS WITH A PICNIC LUNCH FOR FOUR

Honey, Seed and Oat Bars

Rosemary Farinata, Mozzarella,
Pine Nuts and Ratatouille Pickle

Iced Peach Tea

As menu titles go, this one's rather dictatorial! The location is obviously as moveable as the feast but, being a proud Sussex girl who grew up by the South Downs, I know where my walk of choice would be.

HONEY, SEED AND OAT BARS

HANDS-ON TIME: 15 MINUTES

175g runny honey
100g brown sugar
100g crunchy peanut
butter
125ml sunflower oil
175g whole rolled oats
150g porridge oats or
oatmeal
4 tbsp wheatgerm
150g mixed seeds
(sesame, linseed,
sunflower, pumpkin)
100g dried black cherries

Crisp on top, chewy beneath, the oat mixture will cool to the perfect consistency. If you keep the basic proportions the same, the seeds and dried cherries can be swapped for your choice of nuts and/or other dried fruits. Wrap the bars in foil or paper, individually or in small numbers, to transport. Makes 16–20 bars.

Line a 20x20cm square tin with non-stick baking parchment and preheat the oven to 160°C/fan 150°C/325°F/gas mark 3.

Warm the honey, sugar, peanut butter and oil together in a small pan, stirring until combined. Combine all the remaining ingredients in a mixing bowl, pour the honey mixture over and stir well with a wooden spoon.

Press into the tin and bake for about 20–25 minutes, until just turning golden. The mixture will set on cooling. Mark into 16 or 20 bars but leave to completely cool in the tin before slicing. They will keep for a few days in an airtight container.

To make a refreshing **ICED PEACH TEA**, halve and stone two very ripe, fragrant peaches and chop roughly, until the flesh has broken right down. Add 60g caster sugar to 850ml water in a saucepan and bring to the boil. Once bubbling, remove from the heat and stir in two or three Darjeeling tea bags, depending on how strong you like your tea, along with the chopped peaches and their juice. Cover with a lid and leave to steep for three minutes. Strain through a fine sieve, cool, add the juice of half a lemon and chill in the refrigerator. Serve in four tall glasses, over ice, with fresh mint sprigs and a wedge of peach, or pour into a flask ready to drink later.

ROSEMARY FARINATA, MOZZARELLA, PINE NUTS AND RATATOUILLE PICKLE

HANDS-ON TIME: 15 MINUTES

300g chickpea (gram) flour
1 tsp salt
75ml extra-virgin olive oil
2 tbsp finely chopped rosemary leaves
olive oil, for cooking
1 ball buffalo mozzarella, drained and sliced
small handful of toasted pine nuts
about 300g Ratatouille Pickles (see page 148) or char-grilled or roast Mediterranean vegetables, drained of pickling liquid or oil

Should you find yourself making farinata (chickpea flour pancakes) to eat at home, cook them for a bit longer, until really crisp at the edges. Then cut into pieces and serve straight away, with the cheese and vegetables alongside and a drizzle of extra-virgin olive oil over the top. Farinata taste excellent hot or cold; crisp or a little softer.

Put the chickpea flour in a mixing bowl and measure 320ml warm water, the salt and extra-virgin oil into a jug. Gradually pour this into the flour, mixing constantly to prevent lumps forming. The batter should be no thicker than single cream. Pour the whole lot back into the jug, stir in the rosemary and set aside to rest for at least half an hour. You can make the batter a day ahead and keep it cool until needed. Stir well before using.

Heat a little oil in a non-stick frying pan and add a ladleful of stirred batter. Tilt and swirl the pan to create a thin circle, as if you were making a pancake. Cook, over a medium flame, for four minutes on each side, flipping over with a spatula, then transfer to a plate and repeat to make eight golden pancakes. Separate the rounds with pieces of non-stick baking parchment and wrap the whole lot in foil.

Wrap the cheese, pine nuts and pickles or vegetables and pack separately to the pancakes. Sandwich or wrap the salad mix in farinata rounds to eat.

CAMPER VAN (OR CAMPING) BY THE WOODS FOR FOUR

Staffordshire Oatcakes with
Ham and Gruyere

■

Woodland Hash, with a Fried
Egg on Top

■

Stickiest Gingerbread

If you go down to the woods today... take a frying pan, a wooden spoon, some gingerbread, oatcake batter, cheese, ham, eggs, salt, pepper, garlic oil and potatoes with you...

STAFFORDSHIRE OATCAKES WITH HAM AND GRUYERE

HANDS-ON TIME: 30 MINUTES

10g fresh yeast or 1 tsp
  dried yeast
½ tsp caster sugar
175g fine oatmeal
75g wholemeal plain flour,
  sifted
75g plain flour, sifted
½ tsp salt
300ml warm milk
butter, for frying
8 thick slices best-quality
  ham
200g gruyere cheese,
  grated

Staffordshire oatcakes are large and soft, much more like pancakes than oat cakes for cheese. They are delicious rolled up with cheese, baked beans, fried eggs, salad, jam... Probably not all at once, though. Making the batter at home a day ahead would be a good idea; you can put it in a large, screw-top jar and take it with you. If you can't find fine oatmeal, grind normal porridge oats in a blender or food processor for a few seconds to break them down. Makes eight oat cakes.

Dissolve the yeast and sugar in about 175ml warm water and set aside for five minutes.

Combine the oatmeal, flours (tip in the bran from sifting the wholemeal flour, too) and salt in a mixing bowl and add the yeast mixture. Gradually stir in 200ml warm water and the milk to form a batter. It should have the consistency of double cream. Set aside for at least 30 minutes, or cover and chill overnight. Give it a good stir before using.

Place a medium frying pan over the heat and rub with a scrap of butter. When the pan is hot, pour in a small ladleful of batter and quickly swirl around the pan to form a thin pancake. Cook for a minute or so, until golden underneath, then flip over and cook for a minute more. Transfer to a plate and repeat to make about eight oatcakes, piling them up in a stack as you go.

Reduce the heat right down and return a cooked oatcake to the pan. Lay a slice of ham on top and scatter over a small handful of grated cheese. Heat through gently - the cheese should start to melt - then roll up and eat straight away. Repeat until all the oatcakes are filled and eaten.

WOODLAND HASH, WITH A FRIED EGG ON TOP

HANDS-ON TIME: 10 MINUTES

Garlic and Herb Oil (see
  below), or olive oil
350g potatoes, scrubbed
  and cut into small cubes
2 large handfuls of fresh
  porcini mushrooms,
  sliced, or other mixed
  mushrooms, sliced if large
4 very fresh, free-range
  eggs

A crushed garlic clove and a few thyme leaves, added to the pan with the mushrooms, will be more than fine if you haven't made or don't have any Garlic and Herb Oil (see below). I would recommend rustling up the oil though; faffing about with garlic around a camp fire isn't ideal.

Add enough oil to cover the base of a large frying pan and set over a medium-high flame. Add the potatoes, stir to coat and cover with a lid or a layer of foil. Reduce the heat (or raise up from the flames a bit) and cook gently for about 15–20 minutes, giving them a stir now and then. Check to see if the potatoes are tender and cook for a few minutes more if you need to. When they show no resistance to the point of a knife, uncover, increase the heat and sauté until golden all over. Tip on to a plate.

Pour a little more oil into the pan, if necessary, and add the mushrooms. Leave to cook, pretty much undisturbed, for about three to four minutes until golden, then push to the side of the pan and crack in the eggs. Cook until the yolks are done to your liking, then transfer the eggs to plates and return the potatoes to the pan. Quickly heat through with the mushrooms and season. Spoon them on to the plates, beside the eggs.

Pour 200ml good olive oil into a small saucepan and add five peeled and halved garlic cloves and two thyme sprigs. Set over a very gentle heat and warm through for about 15 minutes. The garlic and herbs should not begin to sizzle at any point. Set aside to cool, then strain the **GARLIC AND HERB OIL** into a sterilised jam jar or bottle (see page 89). Keep in the refrigerator until needed and use within a few weeks.

STICKIEST GINGERBREAD

HANDS-ON TIME: 15 MINUTES

125g unsalted butter, cubed
75g muscovado sugar
125g golden syrup
125g black treacle, or more
  golden syrup
280g self-raising flour
2 tsp ground ginger
½ tsp ground cinnamon
½ tsp bicarbonate of soda
½ tsp salt
2 free-range eggs
125ml buttermilk
115g stem ginger in syrup,
  drained and chopped, plus
  3 tbsp of the syrup
2 tsp fresh root ginger,
  finely grated

Why use only one type of ginger when you could have three? This is my very best dark and luscious triple gingerbread, cooked in a square, not a loaf. It's stickier that way. You know this already, but I'm just reminding you: keep the gingerbread, wrapped in foil and cosseted in a cake tin, and it will get even better as the days go by. Perfect for a weekend camping or walking. It won't be so good after a week; you really should have eaten it by then.

Line a 20x20cm square tin with non-stick baking parchment. Preheat the oven to 160°C/fan 150°C/325°F/gas mark 3. Melt the butter, sugar, golden syrup and treacle together in a saucepan over a low heat and set aside to cool slightly.

Sift the flour, spices, bicarb and salt into a bowl. Add the melted butter and syrup mixture, eggs, buttermilk, stem ginger, stem ginger syrup and fresh root ginger. Mix all together thoroughly and pour into the lined tin. Bake for about 50 minutes, until the cake is risen and springy.

Cool in the tin. Wrap up tightly in clingfilm and/or foil and keep for one to three days before eating if you like a really strong, rich flavour. The gingerbread will get darker over time, but it's also lovely straight after baking if you can't wait any longer.

SPRINGTIME CAMPER VAN
BY THE SEA FOR FOUR

Camp Fire-Charred Mackerel with
Red Chicory and Pomegranate

Roast Carrot Houmous

Quick Damper Bread Dipping Sticks

Owning a camper van isn't strictly necessary to
make these recipes, nor is being beside the sea
if I'm really honest. But it would be a lovely way
to spend a spring lunch. The essentials are a legal
camp fire, barbecue, griddle or oven and a frying
pan. Hopefully, you'll be able to supplement those
with a fresh catch of mackerel. Hanging about
where the fishing boats come in - or asking around
- will usually pay dividends. Or you could always
catch them yourself.

CAMP FIRE-CHARRED MACKEREL WITH RED CHICORY AND POMEGRANATE

HANDS-ON TIME: 10 MINUTES

8 small mackerel, the
  fresher the better
a little olive oil
3 red chicory bulbs,
  trimmed and roughly
  shredded
small handful of flat-leaf
  parsley leaves (optional)
2 tbsp pomegranate
  molasses
3 tbsp extra-virgin olive oil
lemon wedges, to serve

Sharp-sweet pomegranate molasses is pretty widely available now. Using it in a dressing is a real boon when you're trying to cut down on ingredients; it has such a rich taste that it needs little embellishment. You can make your own by simmering pomegranate juice down with a touch of sugar until thick and syrupy. Use four large mackerel instead of eight small, if necessary.

Gut and clean the fish but leave them whole. Give them a rinse (in the sea if need be), then make a couple of diagonal cuts in each side, brush with olive oil and season. Either grill on bars set directly over a hot fire or barbecue (they'll need two to three minutes on each side), or sear in a hot frying pan for the same amount of time, turning halfway. The fish should be crisp and even a little charred. Divide between four plates and place a handful of chicory and a few parsley leaves (if you have them) beside the fish.

Combine the pomegranate molasses and extra-virgin oil with a little seasoning and drizzle over the fish and salad. Have lemon wedges to hand for squeezing over.

ROAST CARROT HOUMOUS

HANDS-ON TIME: 20 MINUTES

2 large carrots, scrubbed
  and thickly sliced
1½ tsp cumin seeds
a little olive oil
1 fat garlic clove, roughly
  chopped
400g can chickpeas,
  drained
1 heaped tbsp light tahini
  paste
extra-virgin olive oil
lemon juice, to taste
Quick Damper Bread
  Dipping Sticks (see right),
  to serve

This is one to make in advance and take with you, but you could make a rustic houmous on site, without the carrots, by mashing the chickpeas to a rough puree and stirring in the remaining ingredients. Look out for ethnic brands of tinned chickpeas; they are plumper and more flavourful than the sad little ones found in supermarket branded tins. A better alternative would be to use soaked, dried chickpeas and cook them from scratch, but sometimes there just aren't enough hours in the day.

Preheat the oven to 200°C/fan 190°C/400°F/gas mark 6. Toss the carrots and cumin with the oil and season. Spread out in a roasting tin and cook for about 35 minutes, until soft and charring at the edges. Set aside to cool.

Use the flat of a knife to crush the garlic with a pinch of coarse sea salt. Add to a food processor with the chickpeas, tahini and roast carrots and blend to a coarse puree. Add a glug of extra-virgin oil and a squeeze of lemon juice, then taste and adjust the balance until you're happy.

Serve with Quick Damper Bread Dipping Sticks (see right), or warmed flatbreads.

QUICK DAMPER BREAD
DIPPING STICKS

250g white or wholemeal
  self-raising flour
½ tsp salt
15g butter, softened
120ml milk

These are fun to make if you have the means to take the ingredients, a wooden spoon and mixing bowl with you. Before you start, make sure the camp fire embers are hot and that you have about eight clean and sturdy sticks ready. If you go foraging for these, make sure they aren't from a poisonous plant or tree! The quantities on the left are how you'd make it by the book but, really, where's your sense of advanture?

Measure 2 mugfuls of flour into a large bowl. Scatter with the salt and rub in a large knob of soft butter, if you have it, with your fingertips. Otherwise, use a drizzle of oil, or leave it out. You can do all this at home and take the mixture with you in a plastic bag. To this mixture, add half a mugful of milk and about a quarter of a mugful of water (that's 60ml water, if you're still measuring), stirring as you do so, to form a dough. Don't overmix.

Mould a small handful of the soft dough tightly around the end of each stick and hold near to the hot embers of the fire for about 10 minutes, turning carefully, until the bread is golden all over.

Gingerly slide from the stick and break open, to eat with the houmous. You can also melt a little butter and jam in the hole left by the stick, to eat for afters or tea.

If you prefer, double the recipe and shape the dough into a circular loaf, cut a deep cross in the top, wrap loosely in foil and scrunch together well to seal. Bake in the dying embers of the fire for about 20 minutes. It should sound hollow when tapped underneath. Or shape and then bake on an oiled baking sheet for 25 minutes or so at 200°C/ fan 190°C/400°F/gas mark 6.

HOLIDAY LUNCH FOR
SIX TO EAT OUTSIDE

Lamb, Courgette and
Halloumi Burgers
or Vegetarian Burgers

Special Tomato Salad

Grilled Corn and Sweet Potato
with Fresh Lime Dressing

Raspberry Custard Cake

This is easy, bright food for sunny days. Despite being written with a holiday home lunch in mind - a cottage by the sea with a barbecue, to be exact - all these recipes could easily be made from a camper van kitchen or a barbecue at home. But try to eat outdoors if possible; lunch tastes better that way.

LAMB, COURGETTE AND HALLOUMI BURGERS

HANDS-ON TIME: 20 MINUTES

1 courgette, trimmed and coarsely grated
600g best-quality minced lamb
100g halloumi cheese, coarsely grated
small bunch of mint, leaves shredded
5 tbsp Greek yogurt
squeeze of lemon juice
6 ciabatta rolls, halved
young green salad leaves

Just lamb - use the best you can find, coarsely ground and not too lean for the juiciest burgers - with a few other Greek-ish accents. And Italian bread. Simple.

Pile the courgette into a clean tea towel and squeeze thoroughly to remove the excess water. Shake into a mixing bowl and add the lamb, halloumi and half the mint. Season generously with pepper and not so generously with salt (halloumi is on the salty side), then mix together lightly and shape into six patties. Don't overwork the mixture or you'll make the burgers heavy. Cover and chill overnight, if you want to get ahead.

Stir the rest of the mint into the yogurt with the lemon juice, and season to taste.

Griddle, grill or barbecue the burgers for about four minutes on the first side and three minutes on the second. Toast the cut sides of the bread rolls at the same time.

Sandwich each burger between two toasted ciabatta halves with a spoonful of mint yogurt and a few salad leaves.

To make four similar **VEGETARIAN BURGERS**, grate a courgette and squeeze out the water, as above. Whizz a thoroughly drained 400g can chickpeas to a textured puree in a mini food processor, or mash thoroughly with a potato masher. Add to a mixing bowl with the courgette, 60g grated halloumi cheese, 1 heaped tsp harissa paste, the shredded leaves of half a small bunch of mint, a beaten free-range egg, plenty of pepper, a little salt and about 3 tbsp fresh breadcrumbs, or just enough to bind. Mix well and form into four patties. Cook in a little olive oil, in a non-stick frying or griddle pan, for four minutes on each side, until crisp.

Now is the time for the tomato in Britain and we grow some beauties in late summer. Crisp, juicy, perfumed, sharp, sweet and of practically any colour you care to name, the possibilities are varied, to say the least. It really is worth seeking out something with more personality than a nameless supermarket fruit. Make a stunning **SPECIAL TOMATO SALAD** using a few different varieties. Tomatoes are incredibly easy to grow - all you really need is a sunny spot, a grow bag and a tap - so you can go to town with the seed catalogues. Try using Black Russian, Black Krim, Gardener's Delight, Marmande and, my favourite, Sungold, in a salad with a Calabrian-style oregano dressing to set them off (with a thank you to Francesco Mazzei for the idea). Slice the tomatoes thickly and pile on to a serving plate. Make a simple dressing of red wine vinegar, a smooth extra-virgin olive oil, fresh or dried oregano, salt, pepper and a touch of crushed garlic, if you wish. Spoon over the tomatoes and serve. That's it.

GRILLED CORN AND SWEET POTATO WITH FRESH LIME DRESSING

HANDS-ON TIME: 20 MINUTES

2 large sweetcorn cobs,
  with husks
3 small sweet potatoes,
  peeled and sliced
  1cm thick
5 tbsp good olive oil
finely grated zest and juice
  of 2 limes
1 tsp brown sugar
1 long red chilli, deseeded
  and finely chopped
a few basil leaves, shredded

Don't be shy with the salt in this dressing, as the sweet vegetables need it to balance them out. Cooking the corn and sweet potatoes on the barbecue gives them a delicious, smoky depth the griddle pan can't match.

Peel the corn husks back and remove the silken threads inside. Replace the leaves, dip the whole cobs in water (to stop the leaves burning so fast), shake off the excess and barbecue the cobs over hot coals, or griddle in a smoking hot pan, turning every now and then, until beginning to blacken all over. Remove from the heat and, when cooled slightly, brush the remains of the leaves away. Cut the kernels from the cob with a sharp knife.

Toss the sweet potato slices with 1 tbsp of oil and season well. Barbecue or griddle over fierce heat for about two minutes or so on each side, turning with tongs, and remove to a serving plate with the cut corn. They will be a little bit crunchy but that's fine; they're by no means raw and will stand up better to the dressing for having some backbone. Combine the lime zest and juice, sugar, chilli and remaining oil and season to taste. Pour over the cooked vegetables, scatter with the basil and serve.

RASPBERRY CUSTARD CAKE

HANDS-ON TIME: 20 MINUTES

FOR THE CUSTARD
450ml single cream or
   half milk-half cream
1 vanilla pod, split
   lengthways
2 free-range egg yolks
2 tsp cornflour
2 tbsp caster sugar

This unusual recipe makes 10 fabulous slices of cake. The custard will break through the sponge layer and caramelise at the edge of the tin as the cake cooks; the raspberries will form pockets of sauce. Though not the most refined creation, it is marvellous for picnics, camping or a simple dessert because it needs no icing, filling or adornment. Having said that, more fresh raspberries alongside wouldn't go amiss, especially if you've been to a PYO farm and have a few extra on hand. Transport the cooled cake in its tin and cut into wedges on site. Try flavouring the custard with a very sparing amount of rose or orange blossom water or saffron, for a more exotic touch, then showering the cake with emerald-green, nibbed pistachios.

Start with the custard. Measure the cream into a small saucepan and place over a gentle heat. Scrape the seeds from the vanilla pod using the tip of a sharp knife and drop into the cream, along with the empty pod. Meanwhile, mix the egg yolks, cornflour and sugar together in a heatproof mixing bowl.

When the cream is almost - but not quite - boiling, remove from the heat and pour on to the egg mixture, stirring all the while. Return the whole lot to the pan and cook over medium heat, stirring constantly with a wooden spoon, until the mixture bubbles and thickens. Keep boiling for at least a minute. The cornflour will stop it curdling. Cover the surface with clingfilm or a circle of baking parchment to prevent a skin forming and set aside to cool.

Preheat the oven to 160°C/fan 150°C/325°F/gas mark 3 and place a shelf in the middle of the oven. Butter a 23cm springform cake tin and line the base with non-stick baking parchment. Crush the raspberries roughly with a fork to make them juicy, but not pureed. Stir half the crushed raspberries into the cooled custard and set aside.

Beat the butter and caster sugar together until light and fluffy, using an electric hand whisk. Add the eggs one at a time, beating thoroughly between each addition. Stir in a spoonful of flour if it looks a bit curdled. Sift in the remaining flour and baking powder. Pour in the milk and gently fold the mixture together, adding the remaining raspberries until just combined.

Pour half the mixture into the tin and make a shallow well in the centre with the back of a spoon. Pour the raspberry custard into the centre and spread the rest of the cake batter over to cover. Sprinkle with the demerara sugar and bake for 1 hour or so, until golden but still a bit wobbly in the centre.

Allow the cake to cool in the tin, then chill in the refrigerator overnight, or for at least four hours. Remove from the tin when completely cold; you may need to run a knife around the edge to loosen. Cut into slices and serve with extra fresh raspberries.

FOR THE CAKE

250g unsalted butter, softened, plus more for the tin
300g raspberries, plus more to serve
250g caster sugar
4 free-range eggs
250g plain flour
2 tsp baking powder
125ml milk
4 tbsp demerara sugar

BLACKBERRY GRANOLA MUFFINS

MAKES 12 PLUMP MUFFINS
HANDS-ON TIME: 20 MINUTES

100g unsalted butter,
  melted, plus more
  for the tin
125g plain flour
125g wholemeal plain flour
2 tsp baking powder
pinch of salt
150g light brown soft sugar
250ml fromage frais
  or plain yogurt
1½ tsp vanilla extract
2 large free-range eggs
125g granola cereal
150g blackberries
3 tbsp chopped hazelnuts

What you need when you're out on tour is a cake, or cakes, that can withstand a bit of rough and tumble. A late-summery blackberry muffin is lovely first thing, when you've slept in a tent and can't quite face building a camp fire or going festival-foraging. These are just about wholesome enough to placate anyone who (sensibly) might feel cake isn't strictly breakfast fare. There's a granola recipe in the book (see page 30), but you could use a bought cereal instead. This recipe reminds me of my friend Liz who got into the habit of eating a bowl of granola late at night when finals were on, ostensibly because it would save her time in the morning by getting breakfast out of the way... Clearly that was just a cunning excuse to eat more cereal. Vary the berries according to what's in season, use all white flour or replace the granola with decidedly less breakfasty white chocolate, if you prefer.

Lightly butter a 12-hole muffin tin, or line each hole with a paper case. Preheat the oven to 180°C/fan 170°C/350°F/ gas mark 4.

Sift the flours, baking powder and salt into a large mixing bowl and tip in the bran that won't pass through the sieve. Stir in the sugar. Whisk the fromage frais or yogurt, melted butter, vanilla and eggs together, add the wet ingredients to the dry, along with the granola and berries, and stir quickly until just combined. Don't over-mix; less beating equals lighter muffins.

Spoon the mixture evenly into the prepared tin and sprinkle with the nuts. Bake in the middle of the oven for 20–25 minutes, until golden and risen.

Allow to cool in the tin for five minutes, then transfer to a wire rack. Eat warm or cool. They will keep in a cool place, in an airtight container, for up to three days.

INDOOR PICNIC FOR A RAINY SUMMER'S DAY FOR SIX

RYO (Roll-Your-Own)
Saigon Salad Rolls

Black Rice and Charred Prawn Salad

Thai-Style Peanut Sauce

Passion Fruit Slice

The rub with south-east Asian food is that, while not usually difficult in execution, it does take rather a lot of ingredients to get that hot, sweet, salty, sour balance going on. Rather a lot of ingredients means rather a lot of chopping. But that won't matter too much, because chopping is a therapeutic activity providing you keep your fingers unharmed and, once ingredients have been chopped accordingly, you'll be able to throw these recipes together in minutes. The reward for a bit of prep will be vibrant, seductively fragrant recipes that won't weigh you down after eating.

BLACK RICE AND CHARRED PRAWN SALAD

HANDS-ON TIME: 30 MINUTES

FOR THE RICE
3 fat lemongrass stalks
350g Thai black rice or
  sticky rice

FOR THE DRESSING
160ml canned coconut
  milk
3 tbsp fish sauce
3 tsp caster sugar
1½ tsp sambal oelek (or 1
  red chilli, finely chopped)
thumb-sized piece of fresh
  root ginger, peeled and
  finely grated
juice of 1–2 limes, to taste

FOR THE REST
75g cashew nuts, toasted
2 ripe avocados, stoned
  and cubed
bunch of spring onions,
  finely sliced
large handful of coriander
  leaves, roughly chopped
800g raw, peeled
  king prawns
2 tbsp groundnut oil

I'm not sure this spirited salad comes from anywhere in particular; it's from my notebook, via various south-east Asian locations. It's no less delicious for that, though. Black rice has a fantastically toothsome texture and nutty flavour. Red rice or brown basmati would make good substitutes if you can't find the black. Sambal oelek (or sometimes ulek) is a fiery Indonesian chilli paste. It's widely available to buy in jars and can become quite addictive as an addition to salad dressings, marinades and stir-fries. Mint and/or Thai basil would make good substitutes if you have any coriander-haters present. My brother Ian, one of the afflicted, won't be told it's an acceptable foodstuff; apparently it only tastes of soap.

Top and tail the lemongrass stalks and remove the tough outer layers to reveal the softer core. Rinse and reserve these outer leaves and finely slice the inner part.

Rinse the rice thoroughly in a sieve held under cold running water. Tip into a large saucepan and cover with enough cold water to reach over the knuckle of your upright thumb when you rest the tip of it on the rice. Add the outer lemongrass leaves and a large pinch of salt. Slowly bring to the boil and, once boiling, reduce the heat and simmer gently for 30 minutes. Drain off any excess water that remains in the pan, discard the lemongrass and set the rice aside to cool.

To make the dressing, whisk all the ingredients together except the juice of one lime, then taste. Add more lime juice if you want. Set aside.

Pound the cashews in a mortar and pestle until roughly crushed, or finely chop them instead. Mix half the dressing with the drained rice and spoon into a serving bowl. Fold in the avocado, spring onions and most of the coriander.

Place a griddle pan over a high heat to get smoking hot. Toss the prawns with the finely sliced lemongrass and oil and season. Space the prawns out in the hot pan and cook for a minute or so on each side; they should be pink right through and slightly charred. Don't overcook or they will be tough. Tip on to the salad and partially fold into the rice. Drizzle the remaining dressing over, sprinkle with cashews and finish with the reserved coriander.

The salad here could be worthy of a celebratory dinner if served warm with the prawns piled on top, or skewered and griddled. A **THAI-STYLE PEANUT SAUCE** on the side is gilding the lily, but will elevate the rice above picnic fare and works well with the pan-Asian feel. Toast 150g unsalted, dry-roasted peanuts in a moderate oven until just turning golden. Cool, then transfer to a food processor with half a teacup of water, a fat clove of garlic, a dash of sesame oil, 1 heaped tbsp brown sugar, a dash of sesame oil, a dash of soy sauce, a little chopped chilli, a squeeze of lime juice and a generous dash or two of coconut milk. Blend until a rustic sauce forms. Season to taste with a little salt and thin out with more coconut milk, if necessary. The sauce will keep, covered and chilled, for a couple of days, but bring it to room temperature before serving.

RYO (ROLL-YOUR-OWN) SAIGON SALAD ROLLS

HANDS-ON TIME: 20 MINUTES

FOR THE DIPPING SAUCE (NUOC CHAM)

4 tbsp nuoc mam (Vietnamese) or nam pla (Thai) fish sauce
juice of 2 limes
3 tbsp caster sugar
1 small garlic clove, finely chopped
1 small red chilli, finely chopped

FOR THE SALAD ROLLS

18–24 rice paper rounds
300g firm, marinated or smoked tofu, sliced (optional)
large handful of mixed herb leaves: Thai or common basil, mint and coriander
1 cucumber, peeled and sliced into batons
2 long red chillies, finely shredded
thumb-sized piece of fresh root ginger, peeled and finely shredded
100g fine rice noodles, cooked and refreshed (optional)
handful of garlic chives, in 10cm lengths (optional)
soft English lettuce leaves, to wrap

If I can get help putting lunch together, I'll take it, and these fresh, salady rolls lend themselves perfectly to being part of an ulterior make-your-own lunch motive (because making lots of salad rolls yourself is fiddly). Of course, you should pretend this is all part of the fun and definitely not down to lethargy on your part. All you need do is a bit of chopping (you were warned) and make a dipping sauce, then put all the components out in bowls. The main filling event could be cooked prawns and/or pork or chicken instead of tofu, or just stick with extra crunchy vegetables such as sweet pepper and carrot, if you like. A few fine rice noodles will add more substance to each roll.

Start by making the dipping sauce. Combine all the ingredients in a bowl with 100ml water. Taste and adjust any of the components as you wish. It should be salty, sweet and sour with a kick from the chilli. Divide between a few little bowls.

Half-fill three wide, shallow bowls with cool water. Have all the filling components ready on a chopping board and/or set out in bowls.

To make each roll, dip a round of rice paper in the water for a couple of seconds, then remove to a plate and wait for half a minute or so, until it becomes pliable. Pile some tofu (or your chosen protein), herbs, cucumber, a very little chilli and ginger and perhaps a few cooked noodles on to one end. Go easy – you don't want to overstuff.

Fold the sides over, and begin to roll up tightly to form a fat cigar, enveloping a garlic chive as you go, if using. Wrap in a lettuce leaf and dip in the sauce to eat.

PASSION FRUIT SLICE

HANDS-ON TIME: 40 MINUTES

FOR THE BASE
200g digestive biscuits
60g unsalted butter, melted

FOR THE CHEESECAKE
600g cream cheese
2 free-range eggs,
  lightly beaten
2 free-range egg yolks
1 tbsp cornflour, sieved
250g caster sugar
200ml fresh passion fruit
  juice (the sieved pulp
  from about 12 fruits,
  depending on size)
seeds scraped from a
  vanilla pod, or 1 tsp
  vanilla extract

Admittedly, a cheesecake with a fruit jelly topping is veering towards kitsch, but it's no less delicious for that. You could dispense with the topping and just eat the cheesecake with extra tropical fruit, or even on its own. It's best as a whole cheesecake, topping and fruit experience though. What my Mum would term a Big Ev. Look for really wrinkly, perfumed passion fruit, the riper and thus more shrivelled the better. Sieve out the black seeds for the topping if you prefer a smooth texture. I rather like their crunch and often re-add some to the cheesecake mixture too. Start this a day ahead.

Preheat the oven to 160°C/fan 150°C/325°F/gas mark 3. Line a 20x30cm, 6cm deep, tin or dish with non-stick baking parchment.

Place the biscuits in a food processor and blend until finely crushed. Add the butter and pulse briefly, then press the mixture evenly into the base of the tin. Bake for 10 minutes, then set aside.

Beat the cream cheese in a large mixing bowl until smooth. Beat in the eggs, yolks and cornflour, followed by the sugar and, lastly, the passion fruit juice and vanilla. Don't over-mix, as too much air in the mixture will make the cooked cheesecake more likely to crack.

Pour over the biscuit base and smooth the top with a palette knife. Bake for about 30 minutes, until still wobbly in the centre but not browned on top. Turn off the oven and open the door. Leave the cheesecake in there to cool very slowly for 15 minutes (this minimises the chance of the top cracking, though - aside from aesthetics - it doesn't really matter if that happens). Remove from the oven and set aside to cool completely before chilling for at least an hour.

To make the topping, soak the gelatine in cold water for a couple of minutes to soften. Heat 4 tbsp of the orange juice with the sugar in a small pan until simmering. Remove from the heat, then squeeze out the gelatine and stir into the pan. Add the remaining orange juice and passion fruit pulp or juice.

Chill for 20 minutes, then pour over the chilling cheesecake and return to the refrigerator for at least four hours, preferably overnight. Cut into 12 bars to serve. Ripe mango or pineapple slices alongside are lovely.

FOR THE TOPPING
3 gelatine leaves
200ml freshly squeezed
   orange juice
25g caster sugar
50ml passion fruit pulp
   or juice
mango or pineapple,
   to serve

POTATOES can be left to cook in the smoky embers of a camp fire. Wrap whole baking potatoes or sweet potatoes - you're better off choosing small examples that will cook relatively quickly - in foil and bury at the edge of the fire. Check after 20 minutes or so and move the potatoes further away from the heat if they look charred. Likewise, move them into the fire if they don't appear to be cooking. A medium baked potato will take about 50 minutes and a sweet potato 40. You can also cut any type of spud into chunks, dress with olive oil, add salt and pepper, perhaps some spices and herbs, and wrap in a foil parcel, folding the edges over to seal securely but leaving a little room within the package for steam to circulate and help the cooking process. Bury in the white embers, or place on a grill set over the fire, and cook for about 30 minutes, or until tender.

GREEN CURRY PASTE is a cinch to whip up in advance using a blender, ready to take on any camping or camper vanning trip. Blend 10 deseeded and chopped green chillies, four chopped shallots, three chopped lemongrass stalks, five fat, chopped garlic cloves, a thumb-sized chunk of galangal or fresh root ginger, five kaffir lime leaves, 1 tsp shrimp paste (optional), 1 tsp coriander seeds, 1 tsp cumin seeds, a large bunch of coriander with stalks and roots, 2 tbsp groundnut oil and the zest and juice of a lime. Spoon into a screw-top jar and keep chilled. Use within five days to make quick curries and marinades. Make foil parcels for fish, tofu or chicken, leaving one end open. Add a little coconut milk, salt and 1 tsp of curry paste, then fold the edge over to seal very securely. Either hang over the fire using sturdy sticks to suspend, or bury in the hot embers for about 15 minutes, until cooked, depending on the contents.

Posh **TRAIL MIX**, thrown together from white chocolate chips, dark chocolate chips, crystallised ginger, toasted coconut flakes, whole cashew nuts, whole almonds and dried dark cherries - in whatever ratios suit you best - can prove extremely useful to keep everyone going on long walks, or can be munched instead of supper if it rains and the fire won't light.

Prick the top of a **WHOLE BRIE OR CAMEMBERT** and poke in a couple of rosemary or thyme sprigs. Sprinkle with a little white wine, if you have any. Making sure no plastic packaging remains anywhere, but leaving the cheese in its wooden box, wrap in foil and bake in the embers of the fire for 15 minutes, until completely molten in the centre. Serve with bread or toast for scooping out the cheese.

JAMAICAN BACON CHICKEN is great for barbecues. I'm afraid there's no bacon in or on the chicken. Only a can of beer. But saying beer can (and bacon) in a loud Jamaican accent amuses me. Rub a small chicken inside and out with plenty of salt and pepper, a little olive oil, smoked paprika, ground cumin and crushed garlic. Now drink half the contents of a beer can and sit the bird on top of it. The can should be facing upwards, right up the unfortunate chicken's cavity. Stand your chicken upright on a grid set over the glowing coals, but not flames, of a camp fire or barbecue, using the can and the two chicken legs as a tripod. Tent loosely with foil and cook for 80 minutes or so, depending on the size of the bird. The juices should run clear when the thigh is pierced with a skewer.

Make a **BLACKENED FISH RUB** for camping suppers. In a screw-top jar, mix 2 tbsp each smoked paprika (the sweet kind), dried oregano and English mustard powder with 2 tsp each of ground cumin, coarsely ground black pepper and salt. Add two pinches of cayenne and mix well. This makes enough for 12 people. Lightly coat any fish fillets (trout, salmon, mackerel...) in melted butter or oil, dust with a little spice mix and fry in a dry, non-stick pan until cooked through and blackened in places. Eat with a tomato or Avocado Salsa (see page 181) and grilled sweetcorn.

Any fresh herbs, wild or domestic, will be delicious in a **FRITTATA** (providing you can identify them if picking from the great outdoors). If in any doubt of their safety, just make a plain frittata. Fennel herb, dill, thyme, marjoram, oregano, mint, chives, onions, nettles, chervil, parsley and wild garlic leaves (blanch the latter briefly before use) are all ideal. Lightly beat eight free-range eggs with salt and pepper and two handfuls of chopped herbs. Add a little cheese, if you like. Heat a pat of butter in a large frying pan until foaming, then pour in the egg and cook gently for about eight minutes, until the base is golden. Flip on to a plate and slide back into the pan. Continue to cook for a few minutes more, until just set. Remove from the heat and leave to rest briefly before slicing into wedges.

In a large frying pan, cook a chopped onion in olive oil until softened. Add a generous shake of ras el hanout (Moroccan spice mix), a crushed garlic clove, a handful of roasted pepper strips and a couple of small chorizo sausages, sliced. Cook for a few minutes, until the chorizo has released its oil. Stir in 2 handfuls of torn, country-style bread, and cook until toasted to make **MIGAS**. Divide between four plates and top each with a fried free-range egg. Eat with a dab of harissa, if you can take the heat.

★

SEASONAL
SUNDAY LUNCH

FIRSTLY, LET'S ESTABLISH SOMETHING: I'M NOT SUGGESTING YOU SPEND EVERY SUNDAY MORNING SLAVING OVER A HOT STOVE, OR EVERY SATURDAY SHOPPING FOR FOOD. I AM, HOWEVER, HUMBLY POINTING OUT THAT A HOME-COOKED WEEKEND LUNCH IS A CHARMING TRADITION WORTH PRESERVING, EVEN IF IT'S ONLY A FEW TIMES A YEAR. SO HERE ARE FOUR INDULGENT SUNDAY LUNCHES, ONE FOR EACH SEASON, WHICH MIGHT INSPIRE YOU TO COOK LUNCH AND ENJOY A LAZY AFTERNOON OVER IT, JUST ONCE IN A WHILE. MUCH CAN BE COOKED OR PREPARED IN ADVANCE. THE BEAUTY OF SUNDAY IS THAT, EVEN IF YOU SPEND A FEW LEISURELY HOURS LUNCHING, THERE'S STILL A WHOLE EVENING FOR ALL-IMPORTANT POOTLING ABOUT AND GENERALLY GETTING THINGS DONE BEFORE THE WEEK BEGINS. ALL THE MENUS WILL SERVE 6

AUTUMNAL SUNDAY LUNCH FOR SIX

Caramelised Baby Roots, Feta
and Sweet Lemon Dressing

Slow-Roasted Redcurrant and
Thyme Lamb Shoulder

Glazed Cabbage

Giant Yorkshire Pudding

Pear and Almond Tarte Tatin

A hearty lunch, and rightly so for the time of year, but a nourishing feast rather than over-indulgent. As menus go, this is as moveable as they come, so substitute any combination of starchy vegetables you like in the warm salad of roots and replace the Savoy cabbage with red, or with any other winter greens. A shoulder of pork, traditionally sweet at this time of year from pigs feasting on windfall apples, will respond as tenderly and well as lamb to slow-roasting with wine and robust herbs. Lastly, consider pineapple, English apples or perhaps poached quince, instead of pears, in the tart.

CARAMELISED BABY ROOTS, FETA AND SWEET LEMON DRESSING

HANDS-ON TIME: 20 MINUTES

1 lemon, finely zested, then
  halved across its middle
5-6 tbsp olive oil
leaves from 3 thyme sprigs
1–2 tbsp mild honey,
  such as acacia or
  orange blossom
700g baby root veg such
  as parsnips, carrots and
  turnips, scrubbed
300g butternut squash,
  peeled and cubed
12 shallots, peeled
  and halved
2 tsp cumin seeds
200g feta, cubed
50g hazelnuts, toasted and
  roughly chopped

*Sweet young roots are truly lovely right now and balance
perfectly with the salty feta and sharp lemons. If your
vegetables have grown to the teenage or young adult stage,
halve, quarter or chunk before cooking. If you want to
make this the day before, don't add the feta, dressing or
nuts and keep the veg in the refrigerator overnight. Warm
through in a large frying pan before finishing the recipe.*

Set a very large frying pan or wok (cuts down on washing
up when you brown the veg later) over a medium-low heat
to warm up. Sear the lemon halves in the pan, cut sides
down, until the flesh is a shade darker than golden. Leave
to cool slightly before squeezing the juice into a bowl.

Whisk in 3 tbsp olive oil, the lemon zest, half the thyme
and a little honey, to taste. Season with lots of black
pepper and a very little salt.

Bring a large saucepan of salted water to the boil, add all
the vegetables (except the shallots), and simmer for four to
five minutes. Drain very thoroughly in a colander.

Add 2–3 tbsp oil to the pan or wok with the shallots.
Brown gently, stirring, for 10 minutes, then increase the
heat and add the cumin seeds, the well-drained vegetables,
a dash of honey and the remaining thyme. Continue to
cook for 10 minutes, tossing now and then, until all is
sizzling. Tip into a warm serving bowl and toss the feta
through gently, then sprinkle with the nuts. Spoon over the
dressing and serve warm or at room temperature.

SLOW-ROASTED REDCURRANT AND THYME LAMB SHOULDER

1 large lamb shoulder
(about 2kg)
1 tbsp olive oil
10 garlic cloves, unpeeled
and bruised with the flat
of a knife
1 tbsp redcurrant jelly, plus
more to serve
400ml white wine
5 or so thyme sprigs

I've never really gone along with the fuss surrounding young spring lamb; it has hardly had time to live as its 'season' gets earlier with each supermarket marketing campaign. Autumn lamb is obviously more mature and all that extra time spent outdoors produces a flavour worthy of a long and aromatic roast such as this. The redcurrant jelly adds a touch of sweetness.

Preheat the oven to 170°C/fan 160°C/340°F/gas mark 3½. Rub the lamb with the oil and sprinkle with sea salt and freshly ground black pepper. Sit in a sturdy roasting tin (or big casserole) and add the remaining ingredients along with 500ml water. Cover loosely with foil, seal well around the edges and cook on the middle shelf for four hours or so, until incredibly tender when prodded with a knife. Increase the oven temperature to 220°C/fan 210°C/425°F/gas mark 7, remove the foil and roast for about 20 minutes, until turning golden.

Remove the lamb from the oven (you might want to scoop out and reserve a couple of spoons of fat from the tin to cook your Giant Yorkshire Pudding [see page 77] at this stage), re-cover with foil and forget about it for half an hour while you cook the Yorkshire.

Gingerly transfer the lamb to a warm serving plate, tent with the foil and tilt the cooking tin or dish to spoon off as much fat from the surface as possible. Warm up the remaining pan juices, adding an extra slug of water, if needed, over a low heat and serve with the lamb and extra redcurrant jelly.

GIANT YORKSHIRE PUDDING

HANDS-ON TIME: 15 MINUTES

150g plain flour
2 free-range eggs
125ml milk
2 tbsp fat from the lamb, or
  groundnut oil, or goose fat

This is a man-sized Yorkshire. If you feel like showing off, add chopped herbs, toasted spices or a little grated horseradish or parmesan to the batter.

Sift the flour into a bowl, season with salt and pepper, then gently whisk in the eggs, preferably using electric beaters. Of course, enthusiastic human-powered will do the job, too. Gradually whisk in the milk and 90ml water to form a smooth batter. Alternatively, you can tip everything (including the water) into a food processor and blend until smooth. Transfer to a jug so it's easy to pour.

I tend to use mine straight away without resting, but the batter will sit happily for a few hours. It can even be covered and chilled overnight; just leave at room temperature for a while before using.

Check the oven is set to 220°C/fan 210°C/425°F/ gas mark 7. Pour whatever fat or oil you're using into a 28x35cm-ish roasting tin and place in the oven to warm up for five minutes. Keeping the oil temperature high is important here, so give the batter a good stir and quickly pour it into the tin. Return to the oven and cook for 25–30 minutes, until well risen and golden. Chop into sections and serve sharpish, before it starts to sink.

You could simply steam some greens and serve with butter and black pepper, or make easy **GLAZED CABBAGE:** simmer a small glass of white wine in a saucepan until reduced by half. Add a knob of butter, a small, cored and shredded Savoy cabbage, a grating of nutmeg and a small, grated pear. Cook over a lowish heat for five minutes, stirring occasionally, then increase the heat and simmer briskly for a few more minutes to evaporate the liquid and form a glaze. Season before serving.

PEAR AND ALMOND
TARTE TATIN

HANDS-ON TIME: 40 MINUTES

FOR THE QUICK FLAKY
PASTRY
190g plain flour, plus more
   to dust
a pinch of salt
125g butter, frozen

FOR THE PEARS AND
CARAMEL
6 small, ripe pears
lemon juice
150g granulated sugar
60g unsalted butter
10–12 blanched almonds
vanilla ice cream or crème
   fraîche, to serve

*If the need to make your own pastry escapes you, just use
200g bought all-butter puff or shortcrust. Roll it out thinly
though; stodgy tart bases are a bit much after a big lunch.
And there's no need to be nervous when making caramel.
It's easy, I promise; just hold your nerve and keep your
fingers away from the hot sugar.*

Start with the pastry. Sift the flour and salt into a mixing
bowl. Coarsely grate the frozen butter into the bowl and
use a metal knife to combine it lightly with the flour. Add
1½ tbsp ice-cold water and continue to mix with the knife
until it starts to form a dough, adding a few more drops of
water as needed. Gently bring it together with your hands,
form into a disc and wrap well in clingfilm. Chill for at
least 20 minutes, or up to four days.

Peel the pears and halve from top to bottom. Use a melon
baller or teaspoon to remove the cores. Sprinkle with a
little lemon juice to stop them browning and set aside.

You'll need a 20cm-ish ovenproof frying pan for the next
bit, the sturdier the better, as a good, heavy base will heat
up evenly and prevent any hot spots that could burn your
caramel. Failing a pan that will go in the oven, pour the hot
caramel over the base of a round 20cm pie dish or shallow
cake tin before arranging the pears on top.

Preheat the oven to 200°C/fan 190°C/400°F/gas mark 6
if you intend to cook the tart straight away.

Sprinkle the sugar over the base of the frying pan and
set over a gentle heat. The sugar will melt slowly and you
can help it along by tilting and gently swirling the pan
occasionally. Don't stir it or the sugar will go claggy. When
the caramel looks like Greek honey, remove it from the

heat and quickly stir in the butter (pour into an ovenproof dish or tin at this point if your frying pan can't stand the oven). Allow to cool slightly before packing the pears into the pan, rounded sides down. If you're going to cook the tart at a later time, make sure the pan is completely cold before completing the next step or your pastry could melt.

Roll the pastry out on a lightly floured surface until you can cut out a 23cm diameter circle.

Tuck the almonds into the spaces between the pears and drape the pastry over, tucking it inside the pan all around the edge. Prick several times with a fork, cover and chill for up to 24 hours before cooking, if you need to.

When ready, bake on the floor of the preheated oven for about 30 minutes, until the pastry is golden and crisp. Let it settle for a few minutes before turning out on to a plate with a raised edge (use gloves or a tea towel to protect your hands in case the caramel drips).

Serve the tart warm with ice cream or crème fraîche.

GOT TIME TO SPARE A DAY OR TWO BEFORE?

You can cook the root vegetables, make the Yorkshire batter, assemble the tarte tatin until just before baking and prepare the lamb shoulder until it is ready to go in the oven; everything will keep in the refrigerator for a night or two. The lamb can even be cooked the day before: just spoon off any solidified fat before covering with foil and reheating at 180°C/fan 170°C/350°F/ gas mark 4 for 20 minutes or so.

TIMINGS ON THE DAY

Assuming you want to eat around 2pm...

Start by getting the lamb in the oven; it needs a good few hours so aim to have it cooking by **9AM**. Then you can do something else or go back to bed for a bit...

10.30AM If you didn't get a chance to do any advance prep and you're making your own pastry, now's the time to get the pastry mixed and chilled.

While that's chilling, make the Yorkshire batter and set aside.

Now make the tarte tatin up to the point when it goes in the oven, if you haven't made it already.

12.30PM The root vegetables won't mind being cooked at this point; you can leave them in their pan to heat through just before serving. In fact you can do everything except add the cheese, nuts and dressing; throw them in when you're ready to sit down.

1PM Increase the oven temperature to brown your lamb and remove it from the oven about 20 minutes later. While the lamb rests, heat up the fat for the Yorkshire pud, then get the batter into the oven. Transfer the lamb to its serving plate, get the cabbage cooking and finish off the gravy. Finish the baby root salad on its serving plate and get all hands on deck to take everything to the table. Turn the oven down for the tarte tatin.

When the savoury food is winding down, sling the tarte tatin in to bake and set a timer for 25 minutes.

HOT PLATES

I'm not the greatest fan of microwaves but they can come in useful. Besides melting chocolate and softening the butter I've forgotten to take out of the refrigerator in time, they are good for warming plates if the oven is fit to burst. Sit a cup of water on top of a stack of plates and microwave on high for a minute or two.

WINTRY SUNDAY LUNCH FOR SIX

Pressed Pork Terrine, Pear Relish
and Bagel Thins

Roast Duck, Prunes and Chestnuts
or Wild Mushrooms, Prunes and Chestnuts

Pumpkin Crescents and Classic Mash

Chocolate and Salted Caramel Cups
with Scooping Biscuits

Three points of note here, the first being that
the menu is seriously rich in parts and seriously
delicious in its entirety. The second concerns its
distinct unsuitability for vegetarians and the third,
regarding the terrine, is to alert you to a bit of
advance prep. There are ways around all of these:
1. Eat less later.
2. Replace the terrine with a beautiful, light goat's
cheese and the roast duck with earthy mushrooms
for those who would prefer not to eat meat.
3. If you don't have a minute in the four days before
the lunch, refer to the first part of point 2...

PRESSED PORK TERRINE, PEAR RELISH AND BAGEL THINS

HANDS-ON TIME: 30 MINUTES

FOR THE TERRINE
1.6kg pork belly
300ml dry white wine
2 onions, chopped
2 carrots, chopped
4 fresh bay leaves
20 peppercorns
1.8 litres best chicken stock
200g Parma ham
handful parsley leaves,
  roughly chopped, plus
  more to serve

TO SERVE
3 bagels, very thinly sliced
  horizontally
Spiced Pear Relish
  (see page 89)

Seek out British, free-range pork belly; it's still a cheap cut so won't break the bank and you'll be rewarded with a superior flavour. This is a light terrine and too much fat will weigh it down, so look for a good meaty piece of pork. It takes an awfully long time to cook but the results are worth it and the hands-on time practically non-existent. A good, bought chutney will do nicely if you haven't made Pear Relish, and thin toast can stand in for toasted bagels.

Start with the pork. Preheat the oven to 140°C/fan 130°C/275°F/gas mark 1. Lay the belly in a lidded casserole with everything but the Parma ham and parsley. Gently, gently bring to the boil, skimming to remove any scum. Cover and heave into the oven for five hours or so. When completely tender, transfer the pork to a bowl and strain the liquid into a wide saucepan, discarding the vegetables and aromatics. Place over medium heat and simmer briskly for 20 minutes, until reduced by nearly two-thirds. Cool. Remove the skin, fat and gristle from the cooling pork and discard. Break the meat into large pieces.

Line an 11x24cm-ish terrine tin with clingfilm, then line the insides with Parma ham slices, leaving excess wrap and ham overhanging the sides. Combine the pork with the reduced stock and parsley and season to taste. Pack the mixture tightly into the terrine and fold the excess ham and clingfilm over. Weigh down with baked bean cans, or similar, and chill overnight or for up to four days.

Preheat the grill to medium and spread the bagel slices on a baking sheet. Grill for a couple of minutes, until beginning to brown, then turn and grill for a further minute. They will keep in an airtight container for a week or so. Serve the terrine in robust slices with a pile of bagel thins, extra parsley and a spoonful of relish or chutney.

CLASSIC MASH

HANDS-ON TIME: 5 MINUTES

1.5kg medium, floury
  potatoes: Maris Piper,
  King Edward or the
  slightly waxier Desiree
150–200ml milk, warmed
  through
40–60g unsalted butter

I prefer the nutty mash a baked spud produces, and you get the bonus of crisp potato skins if you drizzle them with oil and salt and return to the oven to toast. But if you'd rather cook on the hob, cut the potatoes into large, even chunks and simmer in salted water until quite tender. Drain very well before peeling and ricing - and this really isn't a smug foodie statement - you'll need a potato ricer to make the best. Whip with milk and butter to create a light mash. I've suggested a smaller amount of butter as duck is so rich, but you might want to be a bit more generous when duck isn't on the menu.

Bake the spuds in the preheated oven (it should be at 190°C/fan 180°C/375°F/gas mark 5 for the last bit of duck-cooking) for an hour, or until tender. Scoop out the flesh and rice or mash with the warm milk, butter and salt and pepper to taste, beating until smooth.

If you can't find a dense, vibrant-fleshed pumpkin variety like Crown Prince or Small Sugar, use faithful old butternut squash to make roast **PUMPKIN CRESCENTS**. Toss deseeded wedges of pumpkin, skin on, with fresh sage, olive oil and balsamic vinegar. Season well, spread them out in a roasting tin and bake at 200°C/fan 190°C/400°F/gas mark 6 for 30 minutes, turning halfway, until golden and meltingly tender.

ROAST DUCK, PRUNES AND CHESTNUTS

HANDS-ON TIME: 20 MINUTES

1 large duck, weighing
  about 2.2kg
olive oil
250g pitted prunes
1 eating apple, sliced
2 red onions, finely
  chopped
2 sage sprigs
200g vacuum-packed
  chestnuts
small wine glass armagnac
  or brandy
900ml good chicken stock
baby spinach, to serve

My roast duck renders the fat away, leaving burnished, crisp skin and tender meat. Apart from splattering your oven with oil, a faster roast often results in dry, tough meat as breast and leg disagree on cooking times, so unless you cook the duck in pieces and batches, this way is a winner. Cook two ducks if you're having this on its own, without the meaty starter and indulgent pud.

Preheat the oven to 170°C/fan 160°C/340°F/gas mark 3½. Remove the wing tips from the duck. Prick the skin of the fatty parts of the bird to encourage fat to render. Remove any solid fat in the cavity (keep it for roasting spuds). Put the wing tips in a sturdy roasting tin and set a rack or scrunched-up foil on top. Rub the bird with oil and sprinkle with sea salt. Lay, breast-side down, on the rack. Chop three prunes and stuff into the cavity with the apple, half the onions and a few sage leaves. Roast for two hours, then pour off the fat and turn the duck. Return to the oven for 30 minutes, then blast it at 190°C/fan 180°C/375°F/gas mark 5 for 30 minutes, until golden.

Meanwhile, heat a dash of oil and soften the remaining chopped onion for 10 minutes. Throw in the chestnuts and cook for five minutes. Add the armagnac and reduce, then the stock and remaining prunes. Simmer for 10 minutes. Set aside. The duck can rest, tented loosely with foil, for half an hour; squash and squeeze the juices from the cavity into the armagnac mixture with the back of a spoon. Pour the fat from the roasting tin, discard the wing tips and place over the heat. Add the armagnac mixture and simmer, scraping to release the good bits. Chop the duck into pieces at the table (probably easiest to delegate that) and eat with the Classic Mash and Pumpkin Crescents (see page 83), pan juices and some wilted baby spinach.

This makes two helpings of **WILD MUSHROOMS, PRUNES AND CHESTNUTS**, but can be doubled. I wouldn't reduce the quantities as it gets fiddly.

Clean 400g mushrooms and slice or halve big ones. Include some with character, such as Portobello or porcini; wild would be even better. Fry in a little olive oil or butter in your largest frying pan. Keep the heat high and don't stir too often; you want them to colour. Tip on to a plate. Reduce the heat and fry a finely chopped red onion in a little olive oil or butter for five minutes until soft. Add a slosh of armagnac or brandy, a finely chopped garlic clove, three shredded sage leaves, a few pitted and chopped prunes and 100g chopped chestnuts. Stir for a couple of minutes. Season, then stir in 2 tsp plain flour. Add 200ml vegetable stock and simmer for a few minutes to thicken. Return the mushrooms. Sprinkle with chopped, toasted walnuts for a bit of crunch.

To be fancier, reduce the stock to 60ml and pile the mushrooms and walnuts along the edge of 4 sheets of filo that you have brushed lightly with melted butter or olive oil. Roll up like a Swiss roll, brush with more oil or butter, put in a roasting tin and bake for 20 minutes at 200°C/fan 190°C/400°F/gas mark 6, until golden.

CHOCOLATE AND SALTED CARAMEL CUPS WITH SCOOPING BISCUITS

HANDS-ON TIME: 40 MINUTES

FOR THE BISCUITS
150g self-raising flour
150g caster sugar
125g unsalted butter
1 free-range egg yolk
sea salt

FOR THE CARAMEL
250g caster sugar
3 tbsp golden syrup
a pinch of sea salt
90g unsalted butter
½ tsp vanilla extract
100ml double cream

FOR THE MOUSSE
200g dark chocolate (at
  least 70% cocoa solids)
2 tbsp milk
1 free-range egg yolk
4 free-range egg whites
a tiny pinch of sea salt
30g caster sugar

A judicious amount of salt is magnificent with both caramel and intense chocolate. Admittedly, this is pretty wicked, but it's cold outside (we'll ignore the fact that you've probably got central heating and don't necessarily need the bolstering effects of this to keep warm). If you're short on time the day before, just buy the biscuits, but this recipe makes about 35 and the raw dough freezes well.

Get the biscuits done at least a day before to make things easier. Preheat the oven to 190°C/fan 180°C/375°F/ gas mark 5. In a food processor, blitz the flour, sugar and butter until the mixture forms coarse crumbs. Add the egg yolk and blitz to form a dough. Knead briefly, shape into a sausage, wrap in clingfilm and chill for 30 minutes or up to three days. Cut into thin discs and space out on a lined baking sheet. Top each with a little rock of sea salt. Cook for eight minutes, until sandy-looking. Set aside to cool.

Make the caramel. Combine the sugar, syrup, salt and 50ml water in a heavy saucepan over low heat. Once the sugar has dissolved, increase the heat and boil, without stirring, for five minutes. The liquid sugar should be a rich amber - think Greek honey - and smell caramelly, but not burned, when ready. Watch it like a hawk. Remove from the heat and, being very careful, stir in the butter, vanilla and cream. Divide between cups or glasses and chill.

For the mousse, melt the chocolate in a bowl set over, but not touching the surface of, a pan of simmering water. Pour in the milk, remove from the heat and whisk in the egg yolk. Set aside while you whisk the egg whites and salt until soft peaks form. Gradually whisk in the sugar. Fold into the chocolate mixture until evenly incorporated, then spoon over the caramel. Chill for at least an hour, or up to 12 hours, and serve with the biscuits and little spoons.

GOT TIME TO SPARE A DAY OR TWO BEFORE?

You can make and/or cook the starter and dessert at least a day or two before. The terrine can be made a full four days in advance and kept in the refrigerator.

ROUGH TIMINGS ON THE DAY

Assuming you haven't done any advance prep apart from the starter and you want to eat around 1pm...

If you start at **10AM,** you can easily have the duck ready to eat by 1.30-ish. Grill the bagel thins for the terrine or goat's cheese, if you haven't already, and get the duck ready and into the oven around 10.30am.

11AM The terrine's done or you're serving goat's cheese instead and you'll have made the biscuits (if you are) so best get on with the rest of pudding. Make the caramel - there's still lots of time - you certainly won't want to eat dessert before 2.30 if you sit down at 1 o'clock. Make the chocolate mousse and spread it out on the caramel base. Chill.

12PM Increase the oven temperature and bung the spuds in for the mash.

12.15PM Ditto the pumpkin crescents. Make the gravy for the duck; you'll finish this while the duck rests. Take the duck out of the oven at 12.30-ish and cover with foil. Finish the gravy.

1PM When the potatoes and pumpkin are cooked, reduce the oven temperature and put plates in to warm up. Serve the terrine or goat's cheese, then disappear to the kitchen for a minute to finish the mash and put the pumpkin on a platter.

1.30PM Reheat the gravy. Serve the main course. Make sure you've got at least one helper and divide the main course and mash between the warm plates. Serve the pumpkin at the table.

2.30PM or whenever. Serve pud.

A LITTLE NOTE FOR MESSY OR PANICKED COOKS

You're not trying to be a superhero or a Cinderella; cooking can be hard work but this is supposed to be fun. It shouldn't always be about washing up and wiping surfaces... so if anyone offers to help serve or clear, accept.

Moreover, if you haven't done any advance prep, call in the troops. It's perfectly reasonable to rope others in to help with table laying/onion chopping.

If you're set on keeping up appearances (and making the rest of us look bad), then at least agree to pile up the dirty saucepans somewhere you can't see them and forget about it all for a bit while you enjoy yourself?

SPICED PEAR RELISH

MAKES ABOUT 3 JARS
HANDS-ON TIME: 40 MINUTES

a pinch of saffron threads
6 large pears, peeled,
  quartered and cored
400g light brown sugar
2 tbsp coarsely grated,
  peeled fresh root ginger
2 fat garlic cloves, chopped
1 red chilli, finely chopped
finely grated zest of
  1 lemon
1 tbsp coriander seeds,
  crushed
320ml cider vinegar

If proper chutney-making scares you and/or you need this straight away, reduce the sugar to 275g and the vinegar to 175ml. Keep all the other quantities the same but only simmer for 20 minutes. Cool and keep, covered, in the refrigerator. Use this fresher version within a month.

To sterilise clean jam jars and lids, run them through the hot wash in a dishwasher, or rinse well and pop into a hot oven for five to 10 minutes, until the water has evaporated.

Soak the saffron threads in a couple of spoonfuls of boiling water for two minutes.

Roughly chop the pears and sweep them into a saucepan with all the remaining ingredients, including the saffron and its water.

Bring to the boil and bubble away for about 30 minutes, stirring often, until the liquid has reduced right down and the fruit is soft.

Spoon into the hot, sterilised jars, screw the lids on tightly and turn upside down. Leave to cool, then turn them the right way up. Store in a cool, dark cupboard for up to six months. Once opened, keep in the refrigerator and use within a couple of months.

EARLY SPRING SUNDAY LUNCH FOR SIX

Cornish Sea Bass, Baked with
Woody Herbs and Mushrooms

Celeriac Gratin

Braised Cavolo Nero

Marshmallow Meringues with
St Clements Cream and Rhubarb

It's safe to assume that early spring will be grey and
wet with the odd sunny day chucked in. This is a
menu of seasonal beauties to cheer; the recipes are
vibrant enough to remedy a muted day. Making
everything on the day shouldn't be a problem
as there's nothing tricky, but the meringues, St
Clements cream and rhubarb can be made a couple
of days early and put together before serving. The
celeriac gratin can be made a day ahead, chilled and
reheated when you need it. Stepford-ish it may be,
but there's nothing like a couple of dishes in the bag
to make everything else easier.

CELERIAC GRATIN

HANDS-ON TIME: 15 MINUTES

300ml vegetable stock
3 large celeriac (about 1kg
  each), peeled, halved and
  finely sliced
1 tbsp plain flour
200ml crème fraîche
3 tbsp kalamata olives in
  oil, drained, stoned and
  roughly chopped
1½ tbsp finely chopped
  rosemary leaves

This looks like an awful lot of celeriac but I promise it'll be about right. Use a sharp knife to pare the skin from each celeriac as thinly as possible, cutting away the rooty bits (they look like the chins of the Ood in Doctor Who).

Preheat the oven to 200°C/fan 190°C/400°F/gas mark 6. Bring the stock to the boil in a wide saucepan, add the celeriac and simmer, covered, for five minutes. Remove to a bowl with a slotted spoon and pour the hot stock into a jug. Whisk the flour and a pinch of salt into the crème fraîche and, when smooth, whisk into the jug of stock.

Drizzle a gratin dish with a little oil from the olive jar and layer up the celeriac and crème fraîche, scattering with olives and rosemary and seasoning with freshly ground black pepper as you go. You shouldn't need salt as the stock and olives are salty enough.

To prepare the simply **BRAISED CAVOLO NERO** - and a large bunch (about 400g) will suffice for six - trim out the central stalks. Roughly shred the leaves and plunge into a pan of salted, boiling water. Simmer for about six minutes. Meanwhile, finely slice a couple of garlic cloves and cook gently in a generous dash of olive oil in a large frying pan. Don't let it colour too much. Drain the cavolo nero well and add it to the garlic. Toss over medium heat for a few minutes, then season well and serve warm. If this sounds too simple, add tinned anchovies and their oil, lemon zest and chilli flakes with the garlic in any combination you fancy. Pancetta or bacon, and perhaps a little crème fraîche, is good too. A similar method works beautifully with cauliflower, purple-sprouting broccoli or other winter greens.

Bake, uncovered, for 40–45 minutes, until bubbling and golden. Leave in a warm place for a good 15 minutes before serving, so the liquid can settle.

CORNISH SEA BASS, BAKED WITH WOODY HERBS AND MUSHROOMS

HANDS-ON TIME: 20 MINUTES

2 fat garlic cloves,
  finely sliced
3 tbsp olive oil
500g spring mushrooms,
  brushed free of any dirt
  and sliced
200ml dry white wine
2 x 1kg Cornish sea bass,
  scaled and cleaned
4 bay leaves, torn
a few thyme sprigs
2 tbsp extra-virgin olive oil

It may not be a conventional roast, but a couple of whole baked fish will make a very fine alternative and won't make everyone feel sleepy afterwards. Get the freshest fish you can. If no sleek bass are available, try bream, trout, salmon or snapper. If you need to get ahead, the mushroom mixture can be fried off and cooled, and the foil parcel assembled, a couple of hours in advance. Keep it chilled until you need to bake the fish.

Preheat the oven to 200°C/fan 190°C/400°F/gas mark 6. Lay two large pieces of foil across a large roasting tin; the foil should be bigger than the tin.

In your largest frying pan, gently fry the garlic in the oil for a minute, but do not allow it to colour. Increase the heat and add the mushrooms (you may need to do this in batches to stop them steaming if your pan isn't big enough). Fry, stirring now and then, for a few minutes. You want some good colour so keep the heat high. Add the wine when the mushrooms have golden edges and simmer down for a minute to get rid of the alcohol. Pour the mushrooms and their juices on to the centre of the foil and season very lightly.

Make three diagonal slashes through the skin of each fish on both sides using a sharp knife. Sit the fish on top of the mushrooms. Season each inside and out, then stick a piece of torn bay leaf and a few thyme leaves into each slash, tucking the remaining herbs in and around. Drizzle with the extra-virgin oil and scrunch the foil together to create a loose but tightly sealed parcel. Bake for 25–30 minutes, until just cooked. To serve, open up the parcel, and use a knife and fish slice to lift sections of fish from the bone. Add a good spoonful of the mushrooms and their juices.

MARSHMALLOW MERINGUES WITH ST CLEMENTS CREAM AND RHUBARB

HANDS-ON TIME: 25 MINUTES

FOR THE MERINGUES
4 free-range egg whites
pinch of salt
125g caster sugar
100g icing sugar
½ tsp cornflour
½ tsp white wine vinegar
½ tsp vanilla extract

The St Clements cream I use here is a touch more tart than some, both to counteract the sweet meringue and make the chilled cream softly scoopable. Clementines, tangerines, oranges (use half an orange to replace a whole mandarin) or any other sweet citrus would all do handsomely in place of mandarins. The pink juice of blood oranges would be particularly pretty and, if you track down lovely examples, serve wheels of the peeled fruit instead of the rhubarb.

Start with the meringues. Preheat the oven to 140°C/ fan 130°C/275°F/gas mark 1. Line a large baking sheet with non-stick baking parchment. Using an electric whisk - handheld or free-standing - beat the egg whites, salt and caster sugar until very dense and holding stiff peaks when you remove the whisk. Now sift the icing sugar and cornflour over and continue to whisk for three to four minutes (it's longer than you think!) until the mixture is very stiff and has a shine to it. Whisk in the vinegar and vanilla, then spoon into six mounds on the baking sheet, leaving plenty of space between each meringue.

Using the back of a spoon, make a dip in the top of each meringue for the cream and rhubarb to sit in later. Bake for about an hour (start checking after 45 minutes), until firm. They won't quite be snow-white anymore but they shouldn't be particularly bronzed. You can get away with making meringues up to two days in advance and storing at room temperature in an airtight container.

Now for the rhubarb: in a covered saucepan, gently poach the fruit, together with the sugar and mandarin juice, for four to five minutes, until just tender. Cool and, if it makes life easier, chill for up to three days before using.

Whisk the cream, sugar and citrus juices and zest together until thick. It should still be floppy rather than firm. Use now or cover and chill for a few hours, if you need to.

When you're ready to eat, top each meringue with a scoop of the cream and some of the neon-pink rhubarb. You could do this on a platter or on individual plates. Either way, shower each meringue with chopped pistachios and they're ready to go.

FOR THE RHUBARB
500g forced (pink) rhubarb, trimmed and cut into 4cm lengths
75g golden caster sugar
juice of 1 mandarin

FOR THE POSSET CREAM
280ml double cream
2 tbsp caster sugar
½ lemon, juice only
1 mandarin, finely grated zest and juice
2 tbsp shelled, unsalted pistachios, chopped

HIGH SUMMER SUNDAY
LUNCH FOR SIX

Stuffed Courgette Flowers; Courgette
and Butternut Agrodolce

■

Very Garlicky Roast Chicken

■

Barley Pilaf

■

Cherry Tart with Jasmine's
Almond Pastry

■

Raspberry Barley Water

If the day of your lunch is forecast to be a scorcher,
cook the chicken and pilaf the evening before - or in
the early morning - and serve cold. Anyone who has
grown their own courgettes will know the moment
when enthusiasm for your relentlessly prolific crop
turns to apathy. An agrodolce, 'sour sweet' with
vinegar and sugar, is the best solution. If you have
some vegetarian guests, halve the chicken recipe
and add cooked chickpeas, lentils or butterbeans
to the pilaf. Because you'll only be able to make a
majestic cherry tart when there's a true glut, it's a
fiercely seasonal joy and all the better for that.

STUFFED COURGETTE FLOWERS; COURGETTE AND BUTTERNUT AGRODOLCE

HANDS-ON TIME: 30 MINUTES

4 courgettes, topped, tailed
  and sliced
1kg butternut squash,
  peeled, deseeded and in
  grape-sized cubes
6 tbsp olive oil
2 garlic cloves, sliced
60g brown sugar
150ml red wine vinegar
leaves from a few basil and
  mint sprigs, shredded
175g mild, soft goat's
  cheese
12 fresh courgette or
  pumpkin flowers

Squash flowers are delicate and delicious when raw, so I often shred them and fold into salads or pasta, or stuff and bake until the edges just sizzle, as here (deep-frying on a sunny day probably isn't the best way to enjoy life). Do check for any creepy-crawly action before filling. If you don't grow your own, the blossoms might be hard to come by; should none be forthcoming at farmer's markets, make a simple salad by combining the agrodolce and crumbled goat's cheese with extra basil leaves. On nippier days, this is rather lovely spooned over slices of grilled country bread that have first been scraped with a halved garlic clove.

Start with the agrodolce because it likes to sit and get to know itself for a bit; a few hours or a couple of days of contemplation will do it no harm. Preheat the oven to 220°C/fan 210°C/425°F/gas mark 7. Toss the courgettes and squash with half the oil and spread out in a large roasting tin. Shower with salt and pepper and roast at the top of the oven for 10 minutes, then turn the vegetables over and roast for another five minutes. Pull the tin out and sprinkle over the garlic, sugar and vinegar. Mix well. Roast for 10 minutes more, until sizzling. Stir and cool, then mix in half the herbs. Chill for up to two days, but bring to room temperature before eating.

Meanwhile, combine the cheese and remaining herbs with a little salt and pepper. Remove the stamens from each blossom and carefully stuff with the cheese, unfurling the petals as much as you can to fill the flowers. You'll need the oven at 180°C/fan 170°C/350°F/gas mark 4 for the squash flowers; cook them when you're nearly ready to eat. Arrange them on a lined baking sheet and drizzle with the remaining oil. Bake for 10 minutes, until just beginning to wilt. Serve warm, with the cooled agrodolce spooned over and around.

VERY GARLICKY ROAST CHICKEN

HANDS-ON TIME: 15 MINUTES

2 x 1.2kg free-range
   chickens
8 garlic cloves, peeled
   and crushed, plus 1
   whole garlic bulb, halved
   horizontally
125g butter, softened
leaves from 4 tarragon
   sprigs, chopped
1 lemon, zested and halved
1 onion, sliced
200ml dry white wine
green salad, to serve

I don't bother carving this neatly; I think it's much nicer hacked into pieces. You've will have heard it many times but that's because it's true: it is worth spending extra on free-range birds. The taste will reward you a hundred-fold.

Dry the chickens thoroughly with kitchen paper and sprinkle with salt. Do this a day or two ahead, if you can, and leave in the refrigerator. It will help the skin to crisp up. Bring the chickens to room temperature. Preheat the oven to 200°C/fan 190°C/400°F/gas mark 6.

Mix the crushed garlic with the butter, half the tarragon, the zest and a generous pinch of sea salt. Carefully loosen the skin over the breasts from the neck end and smear two-thirds of the butter under the skin. Pop the rest inside the birds with the lemon and garlic bulb halves. Spread the onion in a roasting tin large enough for both chickens. Sit them on top, breasts up, and roast for 20 minutes.

Turn the chickens over and roast for a further 20 minutes, until golden. Then turn them the right way up for 10–15 minutes to re-crisp the skin. Transfer to a plate, draining any juices back into the tin, tent loosely with foil and rest for 20 minutes. Spoon the fat from the tin, mash the onion and soft garlic from the bulb halves into the juices and add the wine with a glass of water. Bring to the boil, scraping. Bubble down for a few minutes to boil off the alcohol and thicken. Remove from the heat and stir in the remaining tarragon and any juices from under the chickens. Chop the chickens into joints or pieces and serve with the pan juices, a green salad and Barley Pilaf (see right).

BARLEY PILAF

HANDS-ON TIME: 15 MINUTES

60g butter
1 onion, chopped
250g pearl barley
800ml chicken or
  vegetable stock
150g fresh young peas,
  shelled, or defrosted
  petit pois
2 tbsp finely chopped mint
a squeeze or two of lemon
  juice, to taste

Do swap in pearled spelt or farro for the pearl barley if you wish. The method shouldn't need to change, but do keep an eye on them in case an extra slosh of stock and/ or a little more simmering time is needed. If you've got other summery herbs growing by the kitchen or sitting in the refrigerator, do add them with the mint. Combinations of citrus zest, spices such as cumin and coriander, grated parmesan, toasted nuts or seeds and the like all have a place here, but I like this simple version beside the chicken.

In a large saucepan, melt the butter and soften the onion for about eight minutes, stirring often, until soft and tinged with gold. Add the barley and stir to coat in the butter. Now add the stock and bring to the boil, then reduce the heat right down and simmer gently for about 40 minutes, or until nearly all the stock has been absorbed.

Crush the peas roughly with a potato masher and add to the pan. Cook for five minutes more, until no liquid remains but the peas still have bite. Remove from the heat and stir in the mint and lemon juice with salt and pepper to taste. Serve warm or at room temperature.

RASPBERRY BARLEY WATER

HANDS-ON TIME: 20 MINUTES

500g granulated sugar
a strip of pared lemon zest
60g pearl barley, rinsed
  and drained
225g raspberries
150ml lemon juice (about 4
  lemons)
ice cubes, mint sprigs,
  sliced lemons and
  sparkling water, to serve

Fruit-based barley water makes a great base for cocktails when something a little stronger is called for. This makes about 900ml.

Place the sugar and lemon zest in a large saucepan with 750ml water and bring to the boil slowly, stirring now and then, until the sugar dissolves.

Simmer briskly for five minutes to reduce slightly, add the barley and remove from the heat. Crush the raspberries lightly, tie them up in a square of muslin or a new J-cloth and add to the pan. Leave to infuse and cool for one hour.

Remove the raspberries and discard. Add the lemon juice and pour into a sterilised bottle (see page 89). There's no need to strain the barley water. Drink now, or keep in the refrigerator for a good two weeks.

To serve, pour a little into tall glasses with ice cubes, mint sprigs and slices of lemon. Dilute to taste with sparkling water (and perhaps a slosh of gin or vodka, if the mood takes you).

CHERRY TART WITH JASMINE'S ALMOND PASTRY

HANDS-ON TIME: 25 MINUTES

FOR THE PASTRY
175g plain flour, sifted
¼ tsp fine salt
65g ground almonds
115g butter, diced
80g caster sugar
2 free-range egg yolks
grated zest of half a lemon
   (or ½ tsp vanilla extract,
   or kirsch)

FOR THE FILLING
700g pre-stoned weight
   fresh cherries, stoned
1 tbsp caster sugar
1 small cinnamon stick,
   or a pinch of ground
   cinnamon
2 tbsp redcurrant jelly

FOR THE STREUSEL
80g unsalted butter, melted
80g caster sugar
2 tbsp plain flour
60g flaked almonds

It's nostalgia all the way in this handsome cherry tart. My Mum, Jasmine, always made it for us and the recipe includes the best pastry I've ever tasted: buttery and rich, but light with lemon zest. Should you wish to dispense with the crumble topping and second baking, this is Jasmine version 2: blind-bake the pastry case for 15 minutes and, after simmering the cherries with an extra slosh of water, strain off the juice and simmer with 1 tbsp arrowroot to thicken. Spoon the cherries into the case and spoon over the juices.

Chuck all the pastry ingredients in a food processor with 2–3 tbsp chilled water and pulse until just combined. If it doesn't come together, add a tiny bit more water. Don't over-mix or it will be tough. Press into a 23cm flan ring or dish. (Just break off chunks and spread them out, handling as little as possible.) Trim the edges. Chill for 20 minutes.

Preheat the oven to 190°C/fan 180°C/375°F/gas mark 5 and slide in a baking sheet. Blind-bake the pastry: cover it with baking parchment and fill with baking beans. Place on the baking sheet for eight minutes. Remove the tart, leaving the oven on and the baking sheet in.

Meanwhile, place the cherries in a pan with the sugar, cover and cook on a low heat for five minutes or so, or until juices begin to run. Add the cinnamon and redcurrant jelly, simmer for 2–3 minutes, then set aside.

To protect the pastry, scrunch a strip of foil around the edge of the tart. Fill with the cherries (fishing out the cinnamon stick, if used). With a wooden spoon, stir the streusel ingredients in a bowl until crumbly. Sprinkle over the top and bake for 35–40 minutes, until golden.

MELTING CHOCOLATE CAKE

SERVES 8
HANDS-ON TIME: 20 MINUTES

FOR THE CAKE
150g unsalted butter,
  cubed, plus more for
  the tin
250g good, dark chocolate
  (70% cocoa solids),
  broken into pieces
150g caster sugar
5 large free-range eggs,
  separated
30g ground almonds
1 tbsp bourbon
a pinch of salt

TO SERVE
140ml tub double cream
2 tbsp icing sugar, sifted
1 tbsp bourbon
cocoa powder, sifted,
  to dust

Ah, the wonder of fallen, sunken chocolate cakes. They're rich but oh-so-good and only need a few ingredients. Basically, this is a sinful baked mousse, with only a few ground almonds to take it into cake territory. It might not be the most original recipe, but great chocolate cakes become old friends and this one has saved me on many an occasion. I doubt there's a Sunday lunch in the land it wouldn't round off perfectly.

Lightly butter a 23cm round, springform cake tin, then cut non-stick baking parchment to line the base and sides. Heat the oven to 160°C/fan 150°C/325°F/gas mark 3. Melt the chocolate and butter in a bain marie or in the microwave. Allow to cool a little, then stir until smooth and add 60g of the sugar and 1 egg yolk. Gradually mix in the remaining yolks. Stir in the almonds and bourbon.

Use electric beaters to whisk the egg whites with the salt until they hold soft peaks. Gradually whisk in the remaining sugar, 2 tbsp at a time, whisking until stiff and glossy. Loosen the chocolate mixture with a spoonful of egg white, then fold in the rest with a spatula or large metal spoon. Be gentle; you're trying to retain as much of the volume as possible. Pour the batter into the prepared tin, level the top and bake for 30–35 minutes.

Leave the cake to cool in the tin, on a wire rack, for 15 minutes; it will sink dramatically but this is exactly what's supposed to happen. Remove the sides and leave to cool completely on the base of the tin. Eat, or chill overnight; the texture will become more velvety. Whip the cream, sugar and bourbon until just holding a shape and pile into a bowl. Dust the cake with cocoa and slice at the table.

For those moments when you're pushed for time and need a little something...

Don't ever be scared of simplicity; just make sure your ingredients are excellent. A bowl of the best **FRESH FRUIT** of the season, just as it is, or alongside some fantastic ice cream (no whipped vegetable fat mixes, please!) is more than enough to make a marvellous pudding. Great **CHOCOLATE**, broken into quite large shards and served with good coffee, would be wonderful too. If you feel the need to make something 'proper' to eat after your meal, the following ideas will serve six as written, but they're all quite placid beasts by nature and can be scaled up or down, depending on the size of the crowd you have to feed.

Roll a sheet of ready-rolled, all-butter puff pastry out a little thinner than it comes in the packet and cut into six even rectangles. Space them out on a large baking tray. Slice 100g natural marzipan thinly and divide evenly between the pastry shapes. Slice six ripe figs or eight stoned plums and arrange neatly on top of the **MARZIPAN SLICES**. Drizzle the fruit with a little runny honey and bake at 190°C/fan 180°C/375°F/ gas mark 5 for 20–25 minutes, until the pastry is puffed and golden and the fruit tender and juicy. Serve warm, with plenty of yogurt or crème fraîche.

To make **CARAMELISED BANANAS AND TOFFEE SAUCE,** fry six peeled and thickly sliced bananas in a knob of butter, letting them colour pretty much undisturbed until golden on each side. It should only take two or three minutes. Tip into a bowl and keep warm in a low oven. Return the pan to the heat and add 3 heaped tbsp brown sugar, a slosh of rum, a small pot of single cream and a large pinch of ground cardamom (leave this out if you don't have any to hand). Bring to the boil, stirring, for a minute or two, then stir in a small squeeze of lime juice. Divide the bananas between bowls with ice cream and spoon over the warm sauce. A sprinkle of toasted, chopped pecans would be a cheerful finish.

Use a small food processor or blender to make a dense and rich **CHOCOLATE MOUSSE**: chop 350g dark chocolate into small pieces (or use good-quality dark chocolate chips) and scrape into the processor bowl or blender. Add three free-range eggs with a few drops of vanilla extract or 1–2 tbsp brandy. Bring 220ml milk and 3 tbsp caster sugar to the boil in a small saucepan. Pour the hot milk straight on to the chocolate mixture and blend immediately, for a couple of minutes, until smooth. Spoon into little cups and chill for an hour. Eat with fresh raspberries, if you have any.

A truly ripe Alphonso mango from India is a wondrous thing, but can be elusive outside Britain's spring and early summer months. The tinned Alphonso mango pulp (not the standard insipid tinned mango) - buy it from Asian food shops or some supermarkets - makes a vibrant substitute in a **MANGO KULFI**. Whip a small (140ml) pot of double cream until billowing and loose. Add about 400g fresh or tinned mango pulp (about three fresh mangoes) and 200ml condensed milk and fold together gently. You could also add a little grated lime zest or ground cardamom. Pour into a plastic container, cover with a lid or clingfilm and freeze for at least six hours. Serve scoops with ripe, tropical fruit.

Sprinkle a bowful of Greek yogurt with a layer of dark muscovado sugar. Add a very little ground cinnamon, if you wish, and set aside for an hour. The sugar will melt to form a dark toffee sauce. Swirl through with a large spoon - don't overmix though - and serve the **CARAMEL YOGURT** alongside banana bread, fruit crumbles, tarts, compotes or simple, ripe fruit.

To make **MAPLE SABAYON AND SUMMER BERRIES**, spread a generous handful of summer berries for each person out in a large gratin dish or in individual, heatproof bowls. Separate four free-range eggs, dropping the yolks into a heatproof bowl and saving the whites for meringues (they freeze beautifully in plastic food bags). Add 150ml maple syrup and 100ml white wine to the yolks and set the bowl over a saucepan of simmering water. Using a handheld electric whisk, whip the mixture for about seven minutes, until thick and airy. Spoon over the berries and flash under a hot grill until browned in places.

Baked **CHOCOLATE PUDDINGS,** made in six buttered ovenproof cups, can be conjured from a reasonably well-stocked store cupboard. First preheat the oven to 180°C/fan 170°C/350°F/gas mark 4. Gently heat 125ml milk and 50g cubed butter in a small pan, just until the butter melts. Sift 150g self-raising flour into a large bowl, add 100g light soft brown sugar and 2 tbsp cocoa powder. Make a well in the centre and pour in the buttery milk with a beaten free-range egg, stirring until smooth. Divide between the cups. Now combine another 150g brown sugar with 2 tbsp cocoa powder and sprinkle a sixth over each pudding. Pour 4 tbsp boiling water over each cup (don't fret; it will look a mess) and bake for 30 minutes, until domed and just firm on top. Dust with icing sugar and serve with cream or ice cream; the cunning cake will have formed its own delectable chocolate sauce underneath.

★

SUPPER AND
LUNCH TO SHARE

SUPPER IS FOR SHARING. THERE WILL ALWAYS BE TIMES WHEN DINING ALONE IS A TREAT, AND EVEN A RELIEF; A CHANCE TO EAT CEREAL, ICE CREAM OR TOAST AT AN INAPPROPRIATE HOUR AND WITHOUT DISAPPROVING LOOKS. FOR THE MOST PART, THOUGH, I BELIEVE IN COOKING AND EATING WITH FRIENDS AND FAMILY, AND AN EVENING MEAL IS OFTEN THE ONLY POINT IN THE DAY WHEN LIFE SLOWS DOWN AND TALK TAKES CENTRE STAGE. A SHARED LUNCH IS, SADLY, RATHER A NOVELTY FOR SO MANY OF US THESE DAYS, MOST LIKELY FILED UNDER HOLIDAY OR CELEBRATION. WHEN YOU DO GET THE CHANCE TO ENJOY A LONGER LUNCH, MAKE THE FOOD SHINE. THERE ARE MANY BEAUTIFUL MENUS AND RECIPES HERE TO TAKE YOU THROUGH THE SEASONS.

BUN NOODLE AUTUMN
SUPPER FOR EIGHT

Lemongrass Pork Bun Bowls

Nuoc Cham

The Easiest Frozen Yogurt with a
Blackberry Swirl

This is basically a prep list for a laid-back, barbecued supper. The idea is to get all the main course components ready and laid out in bowls, for everyone to build their own noodles. If that horrifies you (and I'm not quite sure why it would), just follow the method to construct them yourself and ruin everyone's fun, but do include little bowls of dipping sauce and pickles on the table. Follow with the luscious yogurt ice and berries. You could add some amaretti or shortbread biscuits on the side if it feels a bit too light.

LEMONGRASS PORK
BUN BOWLS

HANDS-ON TIME: ONE HOUR

FOR THE QUICK PICKLES
125g caster sugar
250ml rice vinegar
450g carrots, peeled and
  cut into fine matchsticks
200g daikon (mooli or
  white radish), peeled and
  cut into fine matchsticks

FOR THE PORK
1.6kg pork shoulder steaks,
  trimmed
3 red chillies, finely
  chopped
4 garlic cloves, finely
  chopped
4 lemongrass stalks,
  trimmed bulbous 5cm
  only, finely sliced
1 tbsp groundnut oil
3 tbsp fish sauce
2 tbsp caster sugar

FOR THE SPRING ONION OIL
  (OPTIONAL)
75ml groundnut oil
4 spring onions, trimmed
  and sliced

Bun simply means 'vermicelli', but has come to describe this large bowl of vermicelli rice noodles accompanied by dipping sauce, cool salad-y components and warm protein of some sort. Admittedly, this involves a bit of chopping and faffing but, as is my habit, nearly everything can be made in advance and you really can't fail with caramelised pork. It's Vietnamese-style heaven and all the faff will be rewarded. And it won't all be hard graft. If you're of the female persuasion and any of your guests are men, it's very likely you won't be allowed to barbecue the pork yourself anyway. That is just the law of outdoor cooking. When it comes to salad leaves, English or butter lettuce, cos or Little Gem (double the quantity of the latter) are all good candidates. The pickles (do chua in Vietnamese), which can be made with all carrot and no daikon, are incredibly addictive. You'll be adding pickles to everything and I do sometimes wonder how I ever got through life in those dark days before I discovered them.

First, get on with the important business of pickling. Combine the sugar and vinegar with 150ml water and a generous pinch of salt in a bowl, stirring enthusiastically until the sugar dissolves. Add the vegetable matchsticks and set aside for at least two hours. This will keep, tightly covered and chilled, for a good three weeks.

Use a rolling pin to bash the pork steaks out slightly until they're a uniform thickness. About 2cm is good. Mix them with the chilli, garlic and lemongrass in a large dish. Set aside for 30 minutes or chill overnight, if you can.

To make the spring onion oil, if you would like to, pour the oil into a saucepan over a medium heat. When hot, add the spring onions and cook for only 20–30 seconds, until they have wilted. Pour into a bowl and leave to cool and infuse.

Make the dipping sauce (see page 112) and cook the rice noodles according to the packet instructions. Refresh with cold water and drain. Set aside. Get all your salads, pickles, noodles, herbs, nuts and dipping sauce laid out in bowls or plates on the table like an exotic buffet, ready for everyone to help themselves.

Fire up the barbecue if you have one (and it's not raining). The coals should be white hot. When you're nearly ready to eat, add the oil, fish sauce and sugar to the pork and season lightly. Barbecue the steaks for a couple of minutes or so on each side, turning with tongs.

If you're not using a barbecue, place a large griddle pan, wok or frying plan over a high heat and turn on the fans in honour of the fish sauce. Griddle or fry half the pork for about two minutes on each side, until the outside is glazed and caramelised. Don't keep turning it; leave it alone as much as you can to get a good colour going. Cover the cooked steaks with foil and keep warm in a low oven while you repeat with the remaining meat.

Here are your assembly instructions: divide a handful of beansprouts, a few lettuce leaves and a little cucumber between deep bowls. Top with a handful of cooked noodles (they will feel sticky and that's fine), a spoonful of spring onions and their oil (if using), a spoonful of drained pickles, a few herbs and a couple of pork steaks. Sprinkle with peanuts and douse each noodle portion with a little dipping sauce just before eating.

TO SERVE

Nuoc Cham dipping sauce (see page 112)
450g fine rice noodles
300g beansprouts
2 large lettuces, washed and leaves separated
1 cucumber, deseeded and cut into matchsticks
plenty of mint, coriander and perilla/shiso (mustard) leaves (just omit the perilla if you can't find it)
150g unsalted peanuts, toasted and finely chopped

The compellingly delicious dipping sauce/salad dressing **NUOC CHAM** is based on nuoc mam, Vietnamese fish sauce. Versions abound, but this one makes a good, entry-level sauce to be adjusted to taste: gently heat 60g caster sugar with 100ml rice vinegar, 150ml water and 100ml fish sauce, until the sugar dissolves. Do not allow the mixture to boil. Cool. Add the juice of a lime - tasting to see how much you want to add - and stir in one or two finely chopped Thai chillies, depending on how hot you like it. When cooking for a crowd, I'd err on the side of mild and offer more chopped chillies on the side for the braver souls. Ring the changes by adding finely chopped garlic, ginger and/or finely shredded pickled carrot and radish.

THE EASIEST FROZEN YOGURT WITH A BLACKBERRY SWIRL

HANDS-ON TIME: 20 MINUTES

FOR THE BLACKBERRIES
1 fat vanilla pod
300g blackberries,
  plus more to serve
125g caster sugar

FOR THE YOGURT ICE
150g caster sugar
500g thick, natural whole
  milk yogurt
250g Greek yogurt

This yogurt is utterly fabulous and slightly better for you than standard ice cream, I suppose. If you want a richer ice, use just the luscious Greek yogurt. You know this already, but it bears repeating: save the vanilla pod. Give it a quick rinse and dry on the back of the oven; it will scent any sugar if you tuck it into the packet and leave them in the cupboard to get to know each other.

Split the vanilla pod lengthways and scrape out the seeds with the tip of a knife. Warm the blackberries, empty vanilla pod and sugar in a saucepan until the berries start to give up their juices. Crush them slightly with the back of a spoon and leave to cool. Chill until needed.

Meanwhile, beat the vanilla seeds into the sugar and yogurts until evenly mixed. If you have the kit, churn in an ice cream machine according to its instructions. Otherwise, pile the mixture into a large plastic container and freeze for an hour. Every half hour after that, whip the yogurt up with a fork, giving it a really good beating to break any ice crystals down and incorporate a bit of air. Repeat this three or four times.

Spoon the nearly frozen yogurt out of the ice cream machine and into a freezable container when the blades stop churning (if you're not using a machine, this is after a couple of hours, when the yogurt is nearly frozen but still soft enough to scoop easily). Spoon the chilled blackberries over, fishing out the vanilla pod, and swirl in gently. Don't over-mix or you'll have uniform purplish yogurt instead of a swirl. Return to the freezer for a couple of hours or overnight. If you have left it in the freezer for more than a day, allow to soften for a good few minutes before attempting to spoon it out. Eat with extra blackberries.

LIGHT, POST-CHRISTMAS
DINNER FOR FOUR

Cumin-Spiced Baked Bream

◾

Carrot Fritters

◾

Ginger Pachadi

◾

Red Citrus with
Bruléed Sabayon

For owners of a pestle and mortar, this is your time
to shine in spice-crushing class. A heavy jar base
or the side of a wine bottle rolled over a chopping
board will do a similar job. If fritter-making feels
like too much on the day, steamed brown rice
makes a soothing substitute. The carrot batter is
well worth the frying time, though, and makes a
great canapé base or light lunch when topped with
roast chicken, yogurt and mango chutney.

CUMIN-SPICED BAKED BREAM

HANDS-ON TIME: 15 MINUTES

6 black bream, each about
  450g, cleaned
200g thick, plain yogurt
2 tsp cumin seeds, toasted
  and crushed
1 tsp garam masala
2 garlic cloves, crushed
¼ tsp hot chilli powder
juice of ½ lime
crunchy salad leaves,
  separated or shredded,
  to serve
lime wedges, to serve

This yogurt coating is nicely mild, to allow the fish to shine through, but you can ramp up the spice if that's your thing. Sub in bass, thick salmon or trout steaks, gurnard, mackerel or monkfish for the bream, if you prefer. Keep an eye on anything wildly different in size or thickness, though. Even the thickest steaks or fillets will take less time to cook than whole fish. I'm only pointing out the obvious because I care: nothing good ever came of overcooked fish.

Preheat the oven to 220°C/fan 210°C/425°F/gas mark 7. Cut a couple of diagonal slashes across the sides of each fish with a sharp knife. Combine the remaining ingredients (not the salad or lime wedges!), season generously with salt and pepper and rub over and inside the fish. Space the bream out on an oiled baking sheet and cook for about 20 minutes, until browned and crisp. A bit of charring is just perfect; it all adds to the flavour.

Plate each whole fish up with a small heap of salad, a lime wedge, a few hot Carrot Fritters and a spoonful of Ginger Pachadi (see page 116).

CARROT FRITTERS

HANDS-ON TIME: 20 MINUTES

groundnut oil, to
  shallow-fry
500g carrots, coarsely
  grated
1 long red chilli, finely
  chopped (deseed if
  you like)
leaves from half a small
  bunch of mint, shredded
2 tbsp sesame seeds
75g chickpea (gram) flour
2 free-range eggs
½ tsp salt

A long red chilli is likely to be mild so these fritters won't be fiery, just crunchy at the edges and tender within. Test the chilli by trying a tiny bit first, though. Better to scorch your own mouth earlier than everybody else's at supper...

Warm a 2cm layer of oil in a high-sided frying pan set over a medium heat. Mix all the remaining ingredients together in a bowl with 2 tbsp water.

Fry heaped tablespoons of the carrot mixture in the hot oil for about two minutes on each side, turning with a spatula, until golden. You'll need to do this in batches, so ferry the cooked fritters to a baking sheet and stow in the oven for a couple of minutes while you fry the rest (keep an eye on them because the oven will be set very high for cooking the fish).

A soothing pachadi is very similar to a raita, counteracting the spice and chilli it meets on the plate in just the same way. To make a **GINGER PACHADI** for six, mix 300g thick, plain yogurt (just good, honest dairy - no low-fat, no pyrotechnics), with 2 tsp finely grated fresh root ginger, a few shredded mint leaves, the grated zest of a lime and a pinch of salt. Add a small squeeze of lime juice to finish and serve with the fish and fritters.

RED CITRUS WITH BRULEED SABAYON

HANDS-ON TIME: 20 MINUTES

FOR THE FRUITS

2 red grapefruit

3 blood oranges

2 tangerines

FOR THE SABAYON

125ml sweet dessert wine,
  such as muscat

125g light brown sugar

3 free-range egg yolks

2 tsp orange blossom water
  (optional)

Now's the time for really stunning citrus fruit, so choose the best on offer, don't feel you have to listen to my bossiness. About seven fruits will be enough for four people. And speaking of bossing, the bruléeing bit is optional too. Skip it if you want but, if you do, might I suggest that a bit of crunch from some chopped pistachios or walnuts would be just lovely instead?

Cut the tops and bottoms from the citrus fruits, then slice away the peel, following the curve of the sides to remove as little flesh as possible. Now cut each fruit into about five wheels, slicing horizontally. Arrange in a large heatproof serving dish, or four smaller bowls.

Measure the wine, sugar and egg yolks into a heatproof bowl set over a saucepan of simmering water and start to whip with an electric whisk, keeping the water simmering. It will take at least six minutes to form the pale and airy mixture you are after. Remove from the heat and whisk in the orange blossom water, if using. Keep whisking from time to time as the mixture cools a little.

Spoon the sabayon over and around the fruits and either use a blowtorch to caramelise the top or flash under a medium grill for a minute or so. Either way, keep a vigilant watch and stop torching or grilling when the sabayon is burnished in places. Take straight to the table.

SIMPLE WINTRY DINNER FOR SIX

Stir-Fried Shredded Greens

■

Chicken and Ginger Clay Pot

■

Sticky Rice Parcels

■

Beautiful Pomegranate Jelly
with Pouring Cream

The key to a sprightly supper in cold weather
is stimulating and warming flavours. Fresh root
ginger, star anise, chilli and garlic provide the fun
for tender chicken and sprightly greens here, and
everything can be made or prepared in advance.
I usually pour the pomegranate jelly into shallow
bowls or cups to set, but don't let that put you
off going down the wobbly unmoulding avenue...
especially when there's this cunning trick for
turning out jellies: sprinkle water over the serving
plate first. You'll be able to scoot the jelly around.
Ostensibly, this is to make room for any twiddles,
but actually it's because moving jelly is funny.

STIR-FRIED SHREDDED GREENS

HANDS-ON TIME: 10 MINUTES

750g water spinach
or large English
spinach leaves
2 tbsp groundnut oil
3 garlic cloves, finely sliced
2 red Thai chillies,
deseeded and finely sliced
2–3 tbsp fish sauce (nuoc
mam or nam pla)

The greens could be anything from water spinach, robust English spinach, bok choy, pak choy, choy sum or gai lan (Chinese broccoli), but really any leafy green loves a garlicky stir-fry. A good nuoc mam (Vietnamese fish sauce) or nam pla (Thai fish sauce) will both do nicely. Use soy if you don't do fish. A bit of last-minute wokking will be needed here, but you can get everything ready to go an hour or so beforehand.

Rinse the spinach leaves in a colander and shred roughly.

Heat the oil and garlic in a large wok or frying pan (adding the garlic to the cold oil should stop it burning so easily) and add the chillies when it just begins to sizzle. Cook for half a minute or so, then add the spinach and stir to coat.

After a couple of minutes, when the leaves have wilted, sprinkle over the fish sauce. Stand back; it'll be a bit pungent! Season with freshly ground black pepper and serve immediately.

CHICKEN AND GINGER CLAY POT

HANDS-ON TIME: 20 MINUTES

3 tbsp golden caster or
   soft palm sugar
3 tbsp light soy sauce
2 tbsp lime juice
2 tbsp fish sauce
60g fresh root ginger,
   peeled and finely sliced
4 garlic cloves, sliced
3 star anise flowers
2 Thai red chillies, pierced
   but left whole
12 bone-in chicken thighs,
   skinned
200ml chicken stock
4 shallots or 1 red onion,
   sliced
Thai basil or coriander
   leaves and finely shredded
   fresh root ginger, to serve

I don't suppose you'll have a clay pot stowed in your kitchen cupboard. A lidded casserole will be fine. This is a fragrant stew with plenty of broth to soak into the Sticky Rice Parcels (see right), balanced between salt, savoury caramel and gentle heat. If you can, marinate the chicken the day before you cook it, otherwise get it into the marinade as soon as possible. Even 20 minutes makes a difference. To make a vegetarian version, use vegetable stock, omit the fish sauce, up the soy sauce to 5 tbsp and replace the chicken with 500g marinated tofu pieces (the kind that have been fried) and 300g shiitake mushrooms. You'll only need to cook it for 30 minutes.

Start the marinade by making a very quick caramel. In a clay pot or sturdy casserole (one that fits in the refrigerator), dissolve the sugar in 3 tbsp water over a gentle heat. Increase the heat and bubble away until it's the colour of runny honey. Remove from the heat and stir in the soy sauce, lime juice, fish sauce, ginger, garlic, star anise and chillies. Add the chicken and turn to coat. Chill for up to 24 hours or set aside to marinate for 20 minutes.

When ready to cook, preheat the oven to 160°C/fan 150°C/325°F/gas mark 3. Add the stock and shallots to the chicken and slowly bring to the boil on a gentle heat. Cover tightly and cook in the oven for about 75 minutes, until completely tender. Or simmer very gently on the hob for an hour, if you prefer. Either way, check after 30 minutes and add a splash of water if it looks dry.

Season with black pepper and, if necessary, a little salt. Serve, or chill for up to two days before reheating. Eat with Sticky Rice Parcels (see right) and Stir-Fried Shredded Greens (see page 119) to soak up the broth. Sprinkle each serving of chicken with herbs and shredded ginger.

Making **STICKY RICE PARCELS** will save you from last-minute rice disasters. Soak 300g Thai sticky (glutinous) rice in plenty of water for a few hours if you can; overnight is best. The recipe will still work if you can't do this, though. Drain the rice, or just rinse if you couldn't soak it, and tip into a saucepan with 600ml stock or water (you can replace 200ml of it with coconut milk, if you like). Add a generous pinch of salt. Bring to the boil and simmer for eight minutes, then set aside to rest for 10 minutes.

Cut out six pieces of banana leaf or non-stick baking parchment. They should each be a bit longer than A5, or about 15x26cm if you want to get a ruler out. Spoon a sixth of the rice up at the end of each and top with a little chopped spring onion. Fold to make little packages, tucking in the edges as you go. Either tie each up with string or just wrap in a square of foil to secure. Chill for up to 24 hours, or until you're ready to go, then steam the rice over simmering water for 15 minutes. Snip the string, or remove the foil, and let everyone unwrap their own parcels.

BEAUTIFUL POMEGRANATE JELLY WITH POURING CREAM

HANDS-ON TIME: 15 MINUTES

3 tbsp caster sugar
800ml fresh pomegranate
  juice (squeezed
  from about 3 large
  pomegranates)
12 gelatine leaves or
  4 tsp gelatine powder
juice of ½ lemon
single or double cream,
  to serve
pomegranate arials (fleshy
  seeds), to serve (optional)

You'll need to start this the day before. The recipe makes one large, obscenely wobbly jelly, or six person-sized creations. Squeeze the juice from halved pomegranates as if they were lemons, then sieve it to remove any stray pith or seeds. But watch your clothes; that juice doesn't seem so pretty when it's splattered down your best white T-shirt. I should know. In spite of any temporarily ruined clothes, this is my favourite. And I think it might be yours.

In a saucepan set over a low heat, warm the sugar in 300ml of the pomegranate juice until dissolved and steaming, but not boiling.

Soak the gelatine leaves (if using) in cold water for three minutes until soft. Squeeze out the water with your hands and stir into the hot juice until completely melted. If you are using gelatine powder, sprinkle it evenly over the hot juice and stir to dissolve. Add the remaining cold pomegranate juice, lemon juice and 200ml chilled water.

Pour into six bowls, cups or 200ml moulds, or into a large 1.2 litre jelly mould or bowl and leave to cool completely, then refrigerate overnight to set.

Either serve the bowls or cups as they are, or turn out: stand the mould(s) in hot water for a second or two to loosen the jelly, before turning out on to a serving plate that you have sprinkled with a spoonful of cold water. Offer cold pouring cream, double or single as you wish, alongside. And some extra pomegranate arials, if you like.

FIVE SUPPER MENUS FOR TWO TO SHARE

This is a chance to serve a couple of racy, last-minute recipes; those that rely on frying and grilling just before serving. Quite frankly, some could be a nightmare to cook in a domestic kitchen for a large group, but are a pleasure to throw together for a table of two, or even four. Because most of the action revolves around the oven top, everything can be made straight off, with no advance preparation. There are a couple of more relaxed options for leisurely evenings; it's not all frenetic activity. I've suggested a starter or a pudding to bolster each main course. I certainly wouldn't worry about producing multiple courses at supper though, so don't feel bound to the idea.

ROBUST SALAD OF SEARED SQUID WITH SAFFRON DRESSING

HANDS-ON TIME: 30 MINUTES

300g small squid with
  tentacles, cleaned
small pinch of saffron
  threads
2 tbsp olive oil
3 red peppers, deseeded
  and thickly sliced
1 red onion, finely sliced
2 tbsp red wine vinegar
1 small garlic clove, crushed
extra-virgin olive oil,
  to taste
2 tbsp capers, rinsed and
  drained
a small bunch of rocket,
  rinsed and drained

Caramelised peppers add sweetness and colour to this vivacious salad.

Cut the cleaned squid bodies into two lengthways and score them in a cross-hatch pattern. Mix the saffron with 1 tbsp boiling water in a cup. Set aside to infuse.

Heat 1 tbsp olive oil in a frying pan and add the peppers and onion. Cook over medium-low heat for 15–20 minutes, stirring, until softened and beginning to brown.

Meanwhile, make the dressing. To the soaking saffron, add half the vinegar and all the garlic, with enough extra-virgin oil to make a dressing you like. Add a little seasoning to balance - remembering the capers will make this salty - and whisk well with a fork.

Tip the caramelised vegetables into a serving bowl and return the pan to a high heat. Toss the squid with the remaining oil, season and spread out in the pan. Cook for one or two minutes each side, turning with tongs, until the hoods curl up and char at the edges.

Return the peppers and onions to the pan with the remaining vinegar and the capers and heat through for a minute. Return to the bowl, add the rocket and dressing and toss everything to combine. Serve warm, with crusty bread on the side if you want.

Finish with the ripest **NECTARINES**, halved, stoned and eaten in bowls **WITH HONEY AND ROSEMARY SYLLABUB**. Whip 100ml double cream until it thickens, then add a squeeze of lemon, 2 tbsp white wine, a bulging dessertspoon of honey and a pinch of finely chopped rosemary leaves. Whip again, until just holding its shape, and eat.

A little **SHREDDED CABBAGE SALAD** to start or on the side should get you in a Viet mood. Shred half a small white cabbage as finely as you can, discarding the core. Place in a bowl with a peeled and finely grated carrot, a handful of chopped mint and coriander and 1 tbsp or so of chopped, toasted peanuts. Crush a chopped red chilli and half a garlic clove to a paste in a mortar and pestle with a little salt. Add 1 tbsp or so of fish sauce, a large pinch of sugar and 3–4 tbsp rice vinegar. Pour over the cabbage and toss to combine.

VIETNAMESE CHICKEN AND SWEET POTATO CURRY

HANDS-ON TIME: 20 MINUTES

4 bone-in chicken thighs, skinned
1½ tbsp Indian curry powder
2 tsp soft palm sugar or light brown sugar
1 tbsp sesame oil or groundnut oil
2 shallots, roughly chopped
1 fat garlic clove, chopped
1 fat lemongrass stalk, trimmed and chopped
½ tsp dried chilli flakes
1 large sweet potato, peeled and cubed
1–2 tbsp nuoc mam (Vietnamese fish sauce) or Thai fish sauce
400ml can of coconut milk
small handful of coriander leaves
steamed rice, to serve

This is a quick version of ca ri ga (chicken curry) but that doesn't make it any less delightful. Add a little chopped galangal or fresh root ginger and/or torn kaffir lime leaves with the garlic, if you have them to hand. You could also substitute prawns or cubed pork for the chicken. The curry will have more resonance if you can marinate the chicken in the curry powder, sugar and salt for an hour before cooking. Indian curry powder is an authentic addition; it's what they use in Saigon. You'll want steamed rice or a hunk of French baguette with this, too; I tend to go for brown basmati but the bread would be more the done thing.

Coat the chicken pieces in half the curry powder, the sugar and a generous pinch of salt. Set aside.

Heat the oil in a wok and add the shallots, garlic and lemongrass. Stir-fry for a couple of minutes, until softened. Add the remaining curry powder, the chilli flakes and the chicken. Stir-fry for a couple of minutes more.

Now add the sweet potato, 1 tbsp of the fish sauce, the coconut milk and half a wine glass of water. Bring to the boil, then simmer for 15–20 minutes, until the chicken is cooked through. Taste and add a little more fish sauce if it needs it. Scatter with coriander before serving with steamed rice.

Finish with fresh fruit if you need something more, whatever's good and ripe.

PAN-FRIED GURNARD, TAHINI SAUCE AND RAINBOW CHARD

HANDS-ON TIME: 20 MINUTES

FOR THE TAHINI SAUCE
1 fat garlic clove, crushed
  with salt
2 tbsp light tahini
juice of half a lemon

FOR THE FISH
200g rainbow chard or
  Swiss chard, trimmed
olive oil, for frying
2 whole 400g gurnard,
  filleted
1 tbsp sesame seeds,
  toasted
lemon wedges, to serve

Though I've tweaked it over time, the tahini sauce idea is shamelessly borrowed from Sam and Sam Clark's fabulous Moro: The Cookbook. *Light tahini, that nutty paste of sesame seeds, is an incredibly useful jar of magic to have on stand-by. Give it a good mix before using, as it tends to separate. A spoonful or two works wonders on many kinds of bean puree, houmous or dressing. Stir it into yogurt with lemon and parsley to eat with falafel, or use in a garlic-spiked sauce, as here. Ask your fishmonger to fillet the fish and, if you can't find the freshest gurnard, try red mullet. Lastly, do look out for rainbow chard when in season; the stalks are so intensely hued they could almost be fake.*

Combine all the ingredients for the sauce with 3–4 tbsp water, enough to give the consistency of single cream. Taste and season as you see fit.

Rinse the chard. Slice the stalks from the leaves and chop into pieces the length of a small thumb. Roughly shred the leaves. Drop the stalks into simmering water with a hefty pinch of salt and simmer for two to three minutes. Drain and set aside. Add the tahini sauce to the empty saucepan and set over the gentlest heat, just to warm it through.

Warm a little olive oil in a frying pan over a medium heat, season the fish and fry for about four minutes each side, until golden brown. Divide between two warmed plates.

Quickly tip the blanched chard stalks into the frying pan with the leaves and return to the heat. Cook, stirring for a couple of minutes, until the leaves wilt. Add a couple of spoonfuls of the tahini sauce, stir well to heat through and divide the chard between the plates with some more of the warmed sauce spooned over. Sprinkle with toasted sesame seeds and offer extra lemon on the side.

MOORISH

A simple **ARROZ CON LECHE**, essentially a rice pudding, would be just the thing after the light gurnard. Warm 250ml milk in a saucepan with a cinnamon stick, a few wide curls of lemon or orange zest and a tiny pinch of salt. When the milk is nearly boiling, stir in 60g short-grain rice and simmer, stirring often, for 15–18 minutes, until tender. Add 25–40g caster sugar, according to taste, and stir in a couple of teaspoons of butter to enrich. Fish out the cinnamon and zest and grate over a little nutmeg, before serving the rice in warmed bowls with a fruit compote, if you wish.

A VIBRANT SALAD OF DUCK, BLOOD ORANGE AND OLIVE

HANDS-ON TIME: 25 MINUTES

2 plump duck breasts
2 tsp coriander seeds,
  lightly crushed
2 blood oranges
2 tbsp extra-virgin olive oil
1 tbsp sherry vinegar
1 tsp honey
1 garlic clove, crushed
2 handfuls watercress,
  washed and drained
small handful good black
  olives, stoned
small handful flaked
  almonds, toasted

Years ago, Tom Kime, an inspirational chap and very talented chef, taught me to cook duck breasts this way and I've never wavered since; starting with a cold pan will render much of the fat away to leave you with beautifully crisp-skinned duck. Winter salads can be just as bright and vibrant as their summer cousins, the only difference being that you might want a little extra bolster to follow (see right). If a leafy main course doesn't do it for you, fold in some cooked quinoa: toast until golden in a dry pan before simmering in chicken stock.

Preheat the oven to 220°C/fan 210°C/425°F/gas mark 7. Rub the duck breasts all over with sea salt, cracked black pepper and the crushed coriander. Lay, skin-side down, in a cold, ovenproof frying pan and place over a low-ish heat. As the duck cooks, the fat will render and you'll be able to pour it out into a bowl. Keep it chilled and covered, ready to make roast potatoes or rillettes another time.

After 10 minutes or so, the skin should be crisp and golden. Turn the breasts and transfer the pan to the oven for eight to 10 minutes. After eight minutes they will be rare, but not too rare. Transfer to a warm plate and leave to rest.

While the duck cooks, lop the tops and bottoms from the oranges and slice off the skin, following the curve of the fruit. Slice the flesh horizontally into wheels and transfer to a bowl. Pour any orange juice on the chopping board into the pan in which you cooked the duck. Add the olive oil, sherry vinegar, honey and garlic and give it a good old mix.

Slice the duck and pour any collected juices into the dressing. Add the watercress to the oranges with the olives and almonds. Toss the dressing through, scatter the duck slices over and serve.

LUXURIOUS

A CHOCOLATE PUDDING. Or, more specifically, a pudding of chocolate. It's only fitting after that luxurious duck. You could make half the recipe for the chocolate mousse part (forget the caramel) of the Chocolate and Salted Caramel Cups (see page 86) and pile it into two teacups to chill before eating. Best Brownies (see page 182) would be eminently suitable too, especially served warm, with ice cream and a simple chocolate sauce. To make a rich sauce, gently melt 60g dark chocolate pieces in 100ml single cream with a generous teaspoon of golden syrup. Add a dash of rum or brandy if you dare and spoon straight over scoops of vanilla ice cream.

SLOW-COOKED PORK, APPLES AND CARAWAY

HANDS-ON TIME: 15 MINUTES

450g pork shoulder,
  trimmed of excess fat
1 eating apple, cut into
  8 and cored
8 shallots, peeled
250g smallish salad
  potatoes, scrubbed
2 garlic cloves, roughly
  chopped
1 tsp caraway seeds
2 tbsp olive oil
wine glass of dry cider
wine glass of good
  chicken stock

Caraway, pork and apples are one of those truly meant combinations. A long, slow cooking time here, but the entire recipe is very quick to put together. Use all stock instead of a stock and cider mixture if you like, but do use a well-marbled piece of pork shoulder; braised pork needs a bit of fat running through it.

Preheat the oven to 160°C/fan 150°C/325°F/gas mark 3. Cut the pork into 5cm cubes and throw into a gratin dish or roasting tin with the apples, shallots and potatoes.

Pound the garlic and caraway seeds in a mortar and pestle with a generous pinch of sea salt to form a coarse paste. Stir in the oil and pour the whole lot over the pork, apple, shallots and potatoes. Add the cider and stock (about 250ml in total if you're measuring), season with black pepper and mix well, spreading all out evenly. Cover with tin foil and bake for an hour.

Crank up the oven to 200°C/fan 190°C/400°F/gas mark 6 and remove the foil, giving everything a stir. Cook for a further 15–20 minutes, until golden at the edges. Serve with wilted spinach or kale or a little grated raw beetroot, lemon juice and olive oil.

RHUBARB SOUFFLES are not the least bit hard to make. Set the oven to 180°C/fan 170°C/350°F/gas mark 4 and place a baking sheet in the middle to warm up. Then roughly chop 200g of the pinkest rhubarb and stir in 60g caster sugar; heating the two together in a covered pan with a splash of water until just softened. Butter two deep ramekins or ovenproof cups and dust the sides with crushed shortbread or ginger biscuits. In a clean bowl, whisk two free-range egg whites with a tiny pinch of salt until they form stiff peaks. Fold in 1 tbsp caster sugar, 1 free-range egg yolk, 3 tbsp fresh vanilla custard (no powdered mixes please!) and a third of the rhubarb compote. Drop a spoonful of the remaining compote into each ramekin and top with the egg mixture. Flatten off the tops, run your finger around the edge of each to create a groove (this helps the soufflé rise) and bake on the hot baking sheet for 16–18 minutes, until risen and golden. Serve straight away, with extra custard poured into the centres and the remaining compote on the side.

CHILLY SPRING LUNCH FOR FOUR

Easy Dhal Soup

·

Fish Fry

·

Curd Rice

·

Date and Tomato Palm

·

Sticky Banana Bread with Fresh Mango
(and Muscovado Cream for Spreading)

A tricky time of year in which to cook. By now, you might be in need of optimistic flavours and colours, but it's still too early to make food insubstantially light. Time to turn East. The spicing of southern India is warm but fresh, often relying on fragrance rather than heat. That's not to say I've been in any way authentic: the dhal soup is a hotchpotch of styles, the fish recipe comes from Chennai, the 'palm' or fresh chutney from Orissa, the curd rice from Kerala and the banana bread from my British kitchen. No apologies though; together they make a very special and substantial lunch.

EASY DHAL SOUP

HANDS-ON TIME: 15 MINUTES

300g yellow split peas, rinsed
200g can chopped tomatoes
160ml coconut milk
1 onion, finely chopped
2 garlic cloves, chopped
2 tsp cumin seeds, toasted
½ tsp ground turmeric
750ml vegetable stock
lemon juice, to taste
2 tbsp groundnut oil
2 tsp mustard seeds
1 red chilli, finely chopped
(deseed first, if you like)

It might take a while to cook, but there's nothing difficult here. Just chuck it all together and it'll practically take care of itself. It might help, time-wise, to make it a day or two in advance, reheating and tempering the spiced topping just before serving. Leftovers freeze perfectly, too.

Tip the split peas, tomatoes, coconut milk, onion, garlic, cumin, turmeric and stock into a large saucepan and bring to the boil. Simmer, half-covered with a lid, for 40 minutes, giving it a stir now and then until the peas have broken down. Season to taste with lemon juice, salt and pepper. It shouldn't be necessary, but thin with a little water to adjust the consistency if you need to. Heat through again and divide between four warmed bowls.

Meanwhile, heat the oil in a frying pan and fry the mustard seeds and chilli, until the seeds pop and dance. Spoon over the hot soup and eat.

FISH FRY

4 ray (skate) wings, about 250–300g each
1 tsp ground turmeric
2 garlic cloves, crushed
1 tsp peeled, finely grated fresh root ginger
½ tsp mild chilli powder
½ tsp crushed black pepper
2 tsp lemon juice
1 tbsp groundnut oil
25g butter
1 sprig fresh curry leaves

Eating this on the coast of Tamil Nadu in south-east India can't easily be beaten for authenticity; I just wish I'd made a better job of writing notes at the time. It's taken several tries to turn 'Chunks of fish. Skate? Southern spice crust - typical. Charred. Juicy.' into a useful recipe... No matter. I got there in the end and it really is very delicious.

If necessary, trim the ray wings with sharp scissors; enough to tidy them, and remove the frill, which tends to burn at the edges and makes the fish too big for most pans.

Mix the turmeric, garlic, ginger, chilli powder, black pepper and lemon juice in a small bowl. Slather over the fish, rubbing it in well, and set aside for at least 20 minutes, or up to a couple of hours, but not overnight; you want the fish to remain as fresh as possible. Divide the oil and butter between two frying pans. Shake the fish dry and season with salt. Add the curry leaves to the pan, followed by the fish, and fry over a medium heat for five minutes each side, until golden. Turn the flame down if it gets too dark; you want to cook the fish through and get a bit of a crust without burning. Serve with a couple of curry leaves, Curd Rice (see page 138) and Date and Tomato Palm (see left).

To make **DATE AND TOMATO PALM**, a quick, fresh chutney that sings with ginger, heat 2 tsp oil or ghee in a saucepan and fry 2 tsp cumin seeds until fragrant. Add 15g peeled and chopped fresh root ginger, three roughly chopped tomatoes or 200g canned chopped tomatoes, 60g stoned and chopped Medjool dates, ¼ tsp ground turmeric, 1 tbsp brown sugar and a pinch of salt. Cook, stirring, for a good few minutes, until thick. Cool before serving. You only need a little chutney to go with the rice and fish so this makes a small amount. Increase the quantities and keep chilled for up to 10 days, if you like.

CURD RICE

200g basmati rice, rinsed
and drained
½ tsp salt
1 tbsp groundnut oil
1 green chilli, halved
lengthwise
1 tsp mustard seeds
1 sprig curry leaves
200g natural yogurt
small handful coriander,
chopped

This is a simple version of curd (yogurt) rice because it doesn't need to compete with the spiced fish or the punchy chutney. If you want to get more elaborate for another time, try adding grated fresh coconut, grated carrot, cumin seeds and cashew nuts in any combination. If this feels like too much work, what with all the other components, just follow the first paragraph of the recipe for plain basmati rice.

Tip the rice into a saucepan with the salt and 600ml cold water. Bring to the boil, then cover and simmer gently for 10 minutes. Remove the pan from the heat and let it rest undisturbed for five minutes.

Meanwhile, heat the oil in a small frying pan, add the chilli, mustard seeds and curry leaves, cooking until the mixture sizzles and pops.

Fluff up the rice with a fork. Fold the yogurt into the rice with the hot spice mix and the coriander.

STICKY BANANA BREAD WITH FRESH MANGO (AND MUSCOVADO CREAM FOR SPREADING)

HANDS-ON TIME: 20 MINUTES

2 free-range eggs
100g unsalted butter,
    melted
200g dark muscovado
    sugar
½ tsp salt
1 tsp vanilla extract
4 large, very ripe and soft
    bananas, mashed
2 tbsp crème fraîche
200g plain flour
1 tsp baking powder
½ tsp ground cinnamon
150g macadamia nuts,
    lightly toasted and
    chopped (optional)
the ripest mango, peeled,
    stoned and sliced

If you don't want to use nuts (or maybe you balk at the price of macadamias? I know I always do), leave them out or replace with 2 tbsp unsweetened, desiccated coconut. Spring is prime time for the most luscious, honeyed Indian mangoes. If you see boxes of elongated Alphonsos for sale, buy them up and use a couple here. You'll be glad you did.

Line a 1kg loaf tin with non-stick baking parchment. Preheat the oven to 180°C/fan 170°C/350°F/gas mark 4.

Whisk the eggs, melted butter, sugar, salt and vanilla together for three to four minutes, until light and airy. Use an electric whisk to save your arms. Whisk in the bananas and crème fraîche.

Sift the flour, baking powder and cinnamon over and fold in to combine. Fold in two-thirds of the nuts, if using. Pour into the tin, sprinkle with the remaining nuts and bake for about 50 minutes to one hour, or until a skewer prodded into the centre comes out clean. Turn out and cool on a wire rack before slicing. Serve in bowls with slices of ripe mango and the Muscovado Cream (see below).

Before you tackle the cake, make a **MUSCOVADO CREAM**. Stir 2 tbsp light or dark muscovado sugar, the finely grated zest of one lime and half of its juice into 200ml crème fraîche or Greek yogurt. Cover and chill for up to two days, until needed. It makes a lovely sponge cake filling or muffin topping too.

LIGHTEST ELDERFLOWER AND RASPBERRY MERINGUE ROULADE

SERVES 8–10
HANDS-ON TIME: 20 MINUTES

4 large free-range
  egg whites
pinch of salt
250g caster sugar
2 tsp cornflour
1 tsp white wine vinegar
1 tsp vanilla extract
icing sugar, to dust
280ml tub double cream or
  crème fraîche
4 tbsp Elderflower Cordial
  (see page 183)
300g fresh raspberries,
  plus more to serve

It may not be the height of fashion but, in contrast to a conventional pavlova, fluffy, cloud-like meringue cooked in a Swiss roll tin is incredibly quick to cook. And any cracks in the outside really don't matter; I think they're beautiful. You could make this a few hours in advance: roll it up around a sheet of non-stick baking parchment and keep in a cool place until you're ready to unroll, fill and re-roll.

Preheat the oven to 180°C/fan 170°C/350°F/gas mark 4. Line a 23x32cm Swiss roll tin with non-stick baking parchment, cutting it large enough so the paper stands proud of the tin by 3cm.

Whisk the egg whites and salt in a very clean bowl, using an electric whisk if you can, until stiff peaks form. Gradually whisk in the sugar, a little at a time, then whisk for two minutes, until you have a very thick, shiny meringue. Briefly whisk in the cornflour, vinegar and vanilla. Spread into the lined tin and bake for about 20 minutes, until firm to the touch. Cool in the tin.

Place a large sheet of baking parchment on a work surface and dust with icing sugar. Turn the meringue out on to this and carefully peel off the top piece of baking parchment.

Now whip the cream (if it is cream you're using) with the elderflower cordial until it just holds its shape; if you're using crème fraîche, just beat in the cordial. Either way, spread over the meringue, leaving a clear border at the edges to stop the filling splurging out at the sides of the finished roulade. Top with the raspberries in an even layer. Roll up from one of the long sides, using the paper to help form an even log. Transfer to a plate and scatter with extra raspberries. Cut into thick, squidgy slices to serve.

A FADED SUMMER KITCHEN
SUPPER FOR EIGHT

Roast Tomato Gazpacho
with Pesto

■

Beetroot-Cured Side of Salmon
and Waxy Potatoes

■

Aioli and Shaved Fennel Salad

■

White Peach and Very Vanilla Tart

This, both for taste and look, is one of my favourite
menus in the book. Time spent at the stove, on
what's likely to be a sunny day, is limited. The
colours, the lightness, suit a jolly, laid-back party
perfectly. With luck, the night will be warm enough
for you to enjoy your supper outside. You can
make pretty much everything up to three days in
advance... the gazpacho, pesto, cured fish, aioli
and all the components of the tart (case, poached
peaches and pastry cream). On the day you'll only
have to boil potatoes, make a fennel salad, slice the
salmon and put the tart together before serving.

ROAST TOMATO GAZPACHO

HANDS-ON TIME: 20 MINUTES

1.8kg reddest, ripest, late-
  summer tomatoes, halved
2 mild red chillies,
  deseeded and
  roughly chopped
5 tbsp extra-virgin olive oil
a thick slice of rustic bread;
  pain de campagne
  or ciabatta
3 red peppers, preferably
  sweet Ramiro, deseeded
  and roughly chopped
1 red onion, peeled and
  roughly chopped
1 fat garlic clove, crushed
1 large cucumber, roughly
  chopped
3 tbsp sherry vinegar,
  to taste
basil leaves and Pesto (see
  right), to serve

Late August and September bring tomato bliss. Choose the most fragrant vine tomatoes you can grow or buy to elevate this soup. Roasting the tomatoes is not conventional, but intensifies their sweetness further. It's best to make this at least a day in advance, if you can. A good gazpacho needs a long chilling time to make it great.

Preheat the oven to 200°C/fan 190°C/400°F/gas mark 6. Spread the tomatoes, cut sides up, in two roasting tins and tuck the chillies underneath (or they will shrivel and burn). Drizzle with 2 tbsp olive oil, season well with salt and freshly ground black pepper and roast for about 30 minutes. They will be a little charred, which is how they are supposed to be. Set aside to cool. Meanwhile, soak the bread in a glassful of cold water.

Pulse everything except the basil and pesto in a food processor or blender, with 100ml water, until almost - but not quite - smooth. Taste and season with salt and freshly ground black pepper. Add a dash more vinegar, if you want. Chill for at least two hours, but preferably overnight. Up to three days in the refrigerator will only do it good.

If needed, thin out the gazpacho with a little iced water before serving, chilled, in bowls with basil leaves and a spoonful of Pesto (see right) on top.

PESTO

HANDS-ON TIME: 10 MINUTES

leaves from 2 large bunches
  of basil (about 150g)
2 garlic cloves
sea salt
3 tbsp pine nuts
75–100ml extra-virgin
  olive oil

Because of the Gazpacho (see left) it is served with, this doesn't feature any cheese; it seems to be a flavour too far in this case. A couple of tablespoons of freshly grated parmesan, stirred in at the end, will keep traditionalists happy. Treat this sauce with the respect it deserves and it will perk up risottos, pastas, barbecues... jarred pestos shouldn't even bear the same name.

Gently wash and dry the basil leaves if they need it. Using a large mortar and pestle, if you have one, or the flat of a knife, if you don't, crush the garlic to a puree with a good pinch of sea salt. The salt crystals will help break the garlic down. Gradually add the pine nuts and basil to your pestle and mortar as you continue to pound; otherwise, pulse the crushed garlic and basil in a food processor. The texture is up to you - as coarse or smooth as you like - but a splash of water helps things along and lightens the pesto a touch.

Stir in enough oil to loosen the pesto, along with freshly ground black pepper and a little more salt, if needed.

I don't put this in when serving it with the gazpacho but, if you are making pesto for other means, stir in the parmesan now (see the recipe introduction, above).

Store, in a lidded jar, for up to five days in the refrigerator with a film of olive oil poured over the pesto to stop it coming into contact with the air. Stir before using.

BEETROOT-CURED SIDE OF SALMON AND WAXY POTATOES

HANDS-ON TIME: 10 MINUTES

1.2kg very fresh side of
  salmon
2 tbsp fennel seeds
1 tbsp black peppercorns
175g light soft brown sugar
110g rock salt
small bunch of dill,
  chopped
2 small beetroot, scrubbed
  and trimmed
2kg small, waxy potatoes,
  such as Anya, Pink Fir
  Apple or Charlotte
Aioli and Shaved Fennel
  Salad (see right) and
  lemon wedges, to serve

The beetroot stains the cured fish with purply pink and it all looks terribly pretty. The contrast of crisp salad, sweet-salty fish, luxurious aioli and hot potatoes is the thing here but if the evening (or day, should you dare to break the rules and serve this at lunchtime) is just too sultry for hot food, dress the spuds with olive oil and serve cold.

Check the salmon flesh for bones and use tweezers to remove any that were lurking undiscovered. Lay the fish out, skin-side down, in a non-metallic dish. Roughly crush the fennel seeds and peppercorns using a mortar and pestle (or the base of a sturdy jar and a chopping board). Mix with the sugar, salt and half the dill in a bowl.

Grate the beetroot and add to the sugar mixture. Spread all over the flesh of the salmon, tucking a little underneath the fish, too. Cover with clingfilm and weigh down with a baking tin and a couple of cans of beans or such like. Chill for at least 24 hours, or up to three days.

Brush off the marinade, rinse the fish very briefly under cold water and pat dry with kitchen towel. Sprinkle with the remaining dill and chill until ready to serve.

Scrub the potatoes if they need it (don't peel, the skin's the best bit) and boil in plenty of salted water for 15–20 minutes, until tender. Drain and serve hot, just as they are. While they are cooking, lay your salmon on a chopping board, skin-side down, and slice very thinly, at a 20–30 degree angle to the board, starting from the tail end. Serve on a board or platter with lemon wedges. Put the Aioli, Shaved Fennel Salad (see right) and potatoes on the table in bowls for everybody to help themselves.

AIOLI is a dreamy and fail-safe stand-by. Crush a small garlic clove (you can always add more later) with sea salt, using the flat of a knife. Whisk a free-range egg yolk in a bowl to break it down, then start to whisk in 400ml mild olive oil, drop by drop at first. As the mixture starts to thicken, add the oil in a thin trickle, whisking constantly, until thick and wobbly. You may not need all the oil. Stir in the garlic and add salt, pepper and a little lemon juice to lift the flavour. I tend to add a small amount of finely grated lemon zest or a little chopped dill at the end.

To make a simple **SHAVED FENNEL SALAD**, trim any coarse outer layers and root from four bulbs of fennel, reserving the frondy tops, and halve each bulb from top to bottom. Use a very sharp knife, or the slicing blade of a food processor, or a swivel peeler, to cut the fennel into very fine slices. Finely chop the fronds and mix with the sliced fennel. Before eating, dress with a touch of lemon juice, extra-virgin olive oil, salt and freshly ground black pepper. Toss a handful of rocket leaves through to finish.

WHITE PEACH AND VERY VANILLA TART

HANDS-ON TIME: 30 MINUTES

FOR THE TART CASE
250g sweet oaten biscuits
100g unsalted butter,
 melted

FOR THE PEACHES
250g caster sugar
300ml white wine
1 vanilla pod, split
8 firmish white peaches

This tart is heaven and I'd highly recommend making it as is. There are many ways to make life simpler, however. Proper pastry cream is always worth it but soft, whipped cream with vanilla seeds and a touch of sugar is never a bad understudy. If your peaches (and do use yellow if white aren't forthcoming) are too ripe, don't bother to poach them at all, just stone and slice. Or you could always just poach whole peaches as in the recipe to eat with vanilla ice cream and shortbread biscuits.

Blitz the biscuits in a food processor until finely ground. (You can also put them in a strong food bag and crush with a rolling pin.) Stir in the melted butter and press firmly into the base and up the sides of a deep, 23cm tart tin with a removable base. Chill for at least three hours to firm up, or wrap in clingfilm and keep chilled for up to three days.

To poach the peaches, place the sugar, wine, vanilla pod and 300ml water in a large saucepan. Bring to the boil very slowly to dissolve the sugar, and simmer for 10 minutes. Cut a shallow cross in the base of each peach and add to the simmering liquid. Poach gently for five minutes, turning occasionally until just tender, then remove from the pan with a slotted spoon. When they have cooled for a minute, you can peel the skins off and return the peach skin to the pan (it will turn the syrup a pretty blush colour). Increase the heat and boil the liquid down by one-third. Cool and strain, then return the whole peaches and the vanilla seeds - scraped from the pod - to the syrup. The peaches can be chilled overnight to use the next day.

To make the pastry cream, heat the milk, salt and vanilla pod in a pan, but remove from the hob when it starts steaming just before the mixture boils. Set aside to infuse for 20 minutes or so, if you have the time. In a heatproof bowl, whisk the egg yolks and sugar together until pale and thickened. Whisk in the flour.

Remove the vanilla pod from the milk, scrape the seeds back into the pan with the tip of a knife and reheat the milk gently. Pour a little into the whisked egg yolks, whilst whisking, then pour in the rest and return the whole lot to the saucepan and the heat. Bring to the boil and simmer briskly, stirring, for two minutes, until thickened. Lay a circle of non-stick baking parchment or clingfilm directly over the surface to stop a skin forming and allow to cool. It will keep, chilled, for up to three days.

Fold the crème fraîche into the cooled pastry cream. Carefully remove the biscuit case from the tart tin - you can leave the base in place - and transfer to a plate. Spoon the pastry cream in and spread it out. Halve and stone the peaches and arrange, cut sides down, across the tart. Spoon some of the peach syrup over just before serving.

FOR THE PASTRY CREAM
280ml whole milk
tiny pinch of salt
1 vanilla pod, split
3 free-range egg yolks
3 tbsp caster sugar
2 tbsp plain flour
150ml crème fraîche

RATATOUILLE PICKLES

MAKES 4 LARGE JARS
HANDS-ON TIME: 20 MINUTES

1 litre wine vinegar (I use
  half red and half white)
3 tbsp salt
200g granulated sugar
1 tbsp black peppercorns
2 tbsp coriander seeds
2 red onions, cut into sixths
4 red, yellow or green
  sweet peppers,
  thickly sliced
2 firm courgettes, trimmed
  and thickly sliced
2 small, firm aubergines,
  topped, halved and cut
  into thick batons
8 garlic cloves, unpeeled
  but bashed lightly
4 rosemary or thyme sprigs
  or 5 bay leaves

*So-called because they use sunny ratatouille-like
ingredients, albeit in a different guise. Pickled summer
vegetables are a revelation and really are very little trouble
to make. You'll be glad you did when lunchtime, or an
impromptu kitchen supper, rolls around: drizzled with
extra-virgin olive oil and eaten with good cheese or cured
ham, a peppery dressed salad, olives and some lovely
bread, they make a rather wonderful spread. I usually
use large 750ml kilner jars here, but small jam jars look
particularly pretty once crammed to the top with the
vegetables. Just make sure they are fully submerged in the
pickling liquid. If you prefer, you can adjust this recipe
to make a more traditional, Italian-style antipasti by
reducing the sugar to 1 tbsp and draining the vegetables
after simmering. You then need to discard the vinegar
mixture and pot the vegetables up as below, but submerge
them in extra-virgin olive oil instead.*

Warm the rinsed-out jars (and lids) in the oven to sterilise
them (see page 89). Slowly bring the vinegar, salt, sugar,
peppercorns, coriander seeds and 500ml water to the boil
in a large pot, stirring to dissolve the sugar and salt. Once
simmering, add the vegetables, garlic and herb sprigs or
leaves and continue to simmer for five minutes.

Ladle the mixture into the warm jars, seal firmly with lids
and turn the jars upside down to cool.

Keep in a cool, dark place for up to six weeks and, once
opened, keep chilled and use within a month.

Because the following suggestions are all rather amiable characters, they would be eminently suited to a starring role as supper the night before their matinée appearance.

You can do better than soggy tuna on wholemeal. Make too many **MEATBALLS** for supper one night, on purpose. Mix best, coarsely minced beef, finely chopped onion and garlic and a pinch of fresh or dried oregano. Bind with egg and breadcrumbs before rolling into rounds. Brown in olive oil, then simmer in a tomato and red wine sauce for 20 minutes. The next day, spoon the leftovers into a robust bun - something Italianate would be fitting - with fresh basil leaves and grated parmesan. Wrap well and pack some napkins for tomatoey fingers.

Leaves quickly lose heart once dressed so, unless you take a separate dressing in a little jam jar (tiny hotel ones are good), I'd stick to grains and pulses for a **PORTABLE SALAD**. Simmer puy lentils, quinoa or pearled spelt or barley in stock until tender. Fold into a tangle of sliced onions and fennel that you have gently fried until golden. Add chopped parsley and sun-dried tomatoes, roughly crushed, toasted walnuts and a peppery-sweet dressing of wholegrain mustard, balsamic vinegar and olive oil. Thickly sliced Italian sausages, or crumbled feta, stirred in at the end, will stand up to all that robustness. Fabulous hot or cold.

Most **SOUPS** like to sit and get to know themselves for a day or two so, if you've got a flask, or the means to reheat a bowlful, consider a hearty Tuscan recipe. Soak 450g dried chickpeas overnight and rinse well. Cover with a thumb's-length of cold water and bring to the boil. Add a couple of chopped onions, carrots and celery stalks. Follow with a can of chopped tomatoes, four rashers of smoked bacon, sliced, and a sprig of rosemary. Cover and simmer for three hours, until the peas are soft. Puree in a blender and season to taste. Meanwhile, heat good olive oil in a pan and fry slices of ciabatta until golden. Drain on kitchen paper and rasp with the cut sides of a halved garlic clove. Take the bread with you, well-wrapped, and submerge in the hot soup before eating. Drizzle with extra-virgin olive oil too, if you can.

Another **BOISTEROUS SALAD**: toast pine nuts until golden and stir into cooked butter beans (jarred are best), red onions, sliced whisper-thin, the ripest chopped tomatoes and chopped tarragon. Make up a strapping dressing in a lidded jam jar of crushed garlic, a very few dried chilli flakes, wholegrain mustard, good old balsamic vinegar and extra-virgin olive oil. This is even better with rocket or flaked tuna, parmesan or leftover roast lamb or chicken.

Rosemary further brightens a simple, but very good, **LEMON PASTA**. You'll probably have all the ingredients for this idea sitting in your kitchen anyway. Cook 200g linguine in plenty of boiling, salted water, according to the packet instructions. Finely grate 60g parmesan into a large bowl. If possible, warm the bowl through first, or at least make sure it's not arctic. Add the finely grated zest of half a lemon, the juice of 1 lemon, 1 tsp finely chopped rosemary leaves and 4 tbsp extra-virgin olive oil, whisking everything together until combined. Season to taste. Drain the cooked pasta in a colander but don't shake it too thoroughly; rather tip it straight into the large bowl with any water still clinging to it, which will help the consistency of the sauce no end. Toss through with the lemon-rosemary mixture and serve.

Remove the good bits from a **CHINESE ROAST DUCK** in large pieces and warm through in a hot oven to re-crisp the skin. Meanwhile, combine toasted sesame oil (or use light tahini or peanut butter instead), lime juice, a little crushed garlic and/or ginger, soy sauce, chopped chilli and chopped coriander. Toss this through cooked soba noodles with cooked, shredded greens (bok or pak choi are good). Add large shreds of the warmed duck and sprinkle with toasted sesame seeds. To eat cold, don't bother to warm the duck.

Fresh lasagne sheets feel luxurious in a **QUICK CRAB CANNELLONI** for two. Gently simmer two cans of chopped tomatoes with a dash of extra-virgin olive oil and white wine, a pinch of saffron and seasoning for 15 minutes. Meanwhile, combine 250g crab meat with 4 tbsp mascarpone, a few drained sun-blush tomatoes, 2 tbsp grated parmesan and chopped parsley. Season with plenty of black pepper. Cook six fresh lasagne sheets in salted, boiling water for a couple of minutes, drain, refresh under cold water and dress with olive oil to stop them sticking. Roll a sixth of the crab mixture in each sheet and place in an oiled baking dish. Spoon the sauce over and place under a grill for 10 minutes, until toasted at the edges.

An **ASIAN SQUASH SOUP** starts with grilling two halved shallots until blackened in places. Peel away the skin and add to a pan with groundnut oil. Fry gently for five minutes, then add two diced tomatoes and a peeled, deseeded and diced butternut squash. Pour in a can of coconut milk, refill the can with stock or water and add, with a couple of kaffir lime leaves and a handful of coriander. Simmer gently for 15 minutes, until completely tender. Remove the lime leaves and blend until smooth, adding a little fish sauce to taste.

★

PARTY

GREAT FOOD MAKES ANY PARTY. KEEP IT CASUAL: LOTS OF FOOD FOR SHARING, LOTS OF BOOZE AND LOVELY FRUIT JUICES AND PLENTY OF ICE FOR MIXING. GONE ARE THE DAYS OF PRINKY CANAPÉS AND UPTIGHT ONE-UPMANSHIP. ENTICING, COLOURFUL RECIPES THAT GET PEOPLE MAKING, SERVING AND HELPING WILL CREATE A LAID-BACK ATMOSPHERE... AND HELP YOU OUT IN THE PROCESS. IT'S YOUR PARTY AND YOU'RE ALLOWED TO RELAX AND ENJOY IT.

THESE ARE SUBSTANTIAL MENUS FOR SPECIAL PARTIES, NOT NECESSARILY TO BE EATEN (OR DRUNK) SITTING AROUND A TABLE.

AUTUMN FILM NIGHT FOR EIGHT

Parmesan and Pepper Popcorn

Spiced Nuts

Salt-Roast Spuds with Smashed
Herb Crème Fraiche

Butternut and Sage Strata
with Garlicky Toasts

Roast Onions

Toffee-Almond Pears

Cosy, indulgent, sharing food for grazing as you
laze. It won't mind sitting about with you.
For the more outdoor-minded, the recipes would
all work beautifully at a bonfire night party. I'd
probably add mugs of hot soup and some mulled
cider to keep everyone toasty while they
coo at the fireworks.

PARMESAN AND PEPPER POPCORN

HANDS-ON TIME: 5 MINUTES

1 tsp sunflower oil
100g unpopped popping
  corn kernels
60g unsalted butter, in
  small cubes
75g parmesan, finely grated
1 tsp coarsely ground mixed
  peppercorns

Popcorn deserves a bit of a revival. Chuck out any unpopped kernels before serving; they're a bit lethal on teeth if unwittingly chewed.

Measure the oil into a large saucepan, preferably one that has a handle on either side, and place over high heat. Add the corn, cover and listen for the popping.

Once the corn begins to pop, start to shake the pan over the heat and keep shaking constantly until the popping slows down again. Remove from the heat and scatter over the remaining ingredients, adding salt to taste. Put the lid back on and toss everything together thoroughly. Pour the whole lot into a very big bowl, removing any unpopped kernels, and serve straight away.

SPICED NUTS, toasted with a touch of sweet, herb and spice, are just the thing for film-side scarfing. Toast 300g mixed nuts - macadamias, almonds and cashews are a luxurious group - in a dry frying pan. Keep the heat low, shake the pan often and don't leave them for more than a second. A panful of burnt nuts might ruin your day. When fragrant and pale gold, add a drizzle of olive oil, a pinch of chilli powder, a shake of dried oregano and a heaped dessertspoon of light honey. Keep toasting, shaking and stirring, until the nuts are caramelised all over. Tip on to a baking sheet to cool and serve in bowls.

SALT-ROAST SPUDS WITH SMASHED HERB CREME FRAICHE

HANDS-ON TIME: 15 MINUTES

FOR THE POTATOES
2kg coarse rock salt
handful of thyme sprigs
1.5kg whole new or small
   potatoes, scrubbed
   if grubby

**FOR THE SMASHED HERB
   CRÈME FRAÎCHE**
2 garlic cloves
handful of soft herbs
   (mint, chives, basil,
   parsley, oregano)
1 lemon, finely grated zest
   and juice
2 tbsp extra-virgin olive oil
400g crème fraîche

Despite what you might expect, these little spuds don't taste overly salty after cooking. Choose potatoes that really taste of potato; something nutty and wonderful like Pink Fir Apple. After baking in their cloak of herby salt, their skins will be wrinkly and their insides buttery-gorgeous.

Preheat the oven to 200°C/fan 190°C/400°F/gas mark 6. Spread half the salt out in a deep roasting tin and scatter with the thyme. Nestle the potatoes on top and cover with the remaining salt. Bake for about 45 minutes, until tender (check by prodding one with a skewer). The cooking time will obviously vary with the size of your potatoes.

Meanwhile, crush the garlic, herbs and lemon zest in a mortar and pestle with a pinch of salt. Add the olive oil and work to a rough puree. Stir this into the crème fraîche with a squeeze of lemon juice and a little black pepper. (No salt because of the spuds.) Use immediately, or cover and set aside for a bit, until needed.

Brush the salt from the warm potatoes and pile the spuds into a warm bowl. Serve the crème fraîche alongside.

BUTTERNUT AND SAGE STRATA WITH GARLICKY TOASTS

HANDS-ON TIME: 30 MINUTES

500ml milk
a thick slice of sourdough
  bread, diced small
6 large free-range eggs
250g ricotta cheese
1 small butternut squash
olive oil
1 large red onion, finely
  chopped
200g chunky bacon
  lardons
small handful of sage leaves
125g buffalo mozzarella,
  torn into pieces
60g mature pecorino or
  parmesan cheese,
  finely grated

If a glance down at the ingredients below introduces any doubt about the merits of a hearty, bread-lined bake accompanied by more bread, worry not. A few cubes of sourdough give the cooked custard extra body and, once you have smushed a warm spoonful or two on to crisp, Garlicky Toasts (see page 160), all will be understood. This is best made, up to the point of cooking, the day before, which should make matters easier. It's an obvious point, but leaving the bacon out will make this vegetarian-friendly.

Measure the milk into a large bowl and stir in the bread, eggs and ricotta with a little salt and coarsely ground pepper. Don't mix it thoroughly; a few golden streaks of egg yolk are a good thing. Set aside in a cool place.

Preheat the oven to 200°C/fan 190°C/400°F/gas mark 6. Peel and halve the squash, scoop out the seeds and cut into wedges. Toss with olive oil, season and roast in a foil-lined tin for 30 minutes. Meanwhile, cook the onion and bacon in a little oil in a large frying pan. Keep the heat gentle for five minutes until the onion softens, then turn up the flame to get the bacon sizzling. Shred half the sage and add to the pan, stir, then tip into the milk bowl.

Spread half the milk and bread out in a large, oiled gratin dish and nestle in half the squash and mozzarella. Repeat, then scatter with pecorino. Cover and chill, overnight if possible, or bake now if time is short.

Set the oven to 180°C/fan 170°C/350°F/gas mark 4 and bake the strata for 40–45 minutes, until golden and bubbling. Sizzle the remaining sage leaves in olive oil for a few seconds. Drain on kitchen paper and scatter on top of the baked cheese. Get your Garlicky Toasts together (see page 160), ready to spread with scoops of the warm strata.

The most tender **ROAST ONIONS**, naturally sugared at the edges and fragrant with thyme, are both vegetable side dish and sauce. Preheat the oven to 200°C/fan 190°C/400°F/gas mark 6. Peel the skin from eight red onions and cut a deep, vertical cross in each. Cram a small thyme sprig into each cross with a sprinkle of salt and pepper. Sit the onions in a sturdy baking dish, drizzle with extra-virgin olive oil and balsamic vinegar, cover with a layer of foil, sealing it well, and bake for about 50 minutes to an hour, until soft and caramelised. Eat the onions - one per person - as they are or scooped on to Garlicky Toasts with the Butternut and Sage Strata (see page 158).

To seek enlightenment through the medium of **GARLICKY TOASTS**, you'll need to grill or griddle a barrage of slender Italian bread slices - a large loaf of sourdough, ciabatta or the like should do it - until a little charred in places. Rub the hot, crisp toast surfaces with a halved garlic clove, and drizzle with a little of your best olive oil. Pile up on a board beside the Strata.

TOFFEE-ALMOND PEARS

HANDS-ON TIME: 20 MINUTES

8 sturdy sticks, cleaned
8 large English pears, well-
 scrubbed to remove any
 wax residue
a little flavourless oil
150g toasted flaked
 almonds
475g light muscovado
 sugar
60g unsalted butter
3 tsp white wine vinegar
3 tbsp golden syrup

How ripe these pears are is up to you; crunchy or juicy both work beautifully with the toffee and nuts.

In the least violent manner possible, stab a stick right into the top (stalk end) of each peaceful pear and line them up, ready for dipping. Smear a little oil over a sheet of foil and use it to cover a baking tray. Locate your sugar thermometer if you have one, but don't panic if you don't.

Spread the almonds out on a small plate and set aside. Put the sugar in a heavy-based pan with 100ml cold water and heat gently, stirring until the sugar dissolves. Increase the heat and bring to the boil. Add the butter, vinegar and syrup but don't stir any more or the sugar might crystallise.

Keep the mixture simmering boldly for about 20 minutes until it reaches the 'soft-crack' stage. To test for this, it's when the mixture reaches 138°C (280°F) on a sugar thermometer. To test for it freestyle, scoop out a tiny bit of toffee with a spoon and drop it into a glass of cold water. You will be able to pull it apart into soft threads between your fingers when the soft-crack stage has been reached.

Remove the pan from the heat and, holding the sticks, quickly dip the pears into the toffee, turning to coat, then roll the bases in the flaked almonds and leave to set on the oiled foil in a cool place (not the refrigerator), for about 15 minutes before eating. Do eat them within a couple of hours or they'll go sticky.

A TERRIBLY CHIC DRINKS PARTY
FOR A WINTER'S NIGHT

Cumin-Spiced Lamb Skewers
with a Fresh Chutney

Sweet Potato Samosas

Sticky Tamarind Chicken Wings

Rice Pudding Squares with
Star Anise Plums

Orange Blossom Mimosas

Light and Stormies

There's a vaguely Asian theme going on this evening;
it seemed apt for an elegant winter's night. Assuming
you'll have about 12 thirsty guests, the following
spread will feed them well. You might want to add a
simple green salad on the side, as this is small plate
food anyway. If the drinks are more the thing - and
they probably will be - make sure there's plenty of
wine and this quantity will stretch to feed 18, even 24
at a push. There are a few tips in the recipes on how
to do this sneakily without anyone noticing.

CUMIN-SPICED LAMB SKEWERS WITH A FRESH CHUTNEY

HANDS-ON TIME: 20 MINUTES

FOR THE SKEWERS

1.2kg cubed lamb leg
2 tsp coriander seeds
3 tsp cumin seeds
3 fat garlic cloves, crushed
200g thick Greek yogurt
2 tsp brown sugar
2 tbsp sunflower oil, plus
  more for baking sheets
small bunch of mint, leaves
  finely chopped, plus more
  to serve

FOR THE FRESH CHUTNEY

2 large, ripe mangoes,
  peeled and finely diced
2 red chillies, finely
  chopped
finely grated zest and juice
  of 1 lime
2 tsp brown sugar

Stretch this to feed more by using large cubes of lamb, removing them from their skewers once cooked and piling up on plates with the chutney and an espresso cup of cocktail sticks alongside. Scatter the extra mint over each plate to pretty it up a bit. Stingier than serving two or three cubes on a skewer, but it will go further... Makes 24–26

Soak 24–36 wooden skewers in cold water for at least 30 minutes. This should stop them scorching under the grill.

Put the lamb in a large mixing bowl. Toast the coriander and cumin seeds in a dry frying pan until fragrant. Tip into a pestle and mortar and crush roughly. Sprinkle over the lamb, using your hands to work the spices into the meat with the garlic, yogurt, sugar, oil and two-thirds of the mint. Leave to marinate for a couple of hours, or chill overnight, if you can.

Combine all the fresh chutney ingredients and stir in the remaining chopped mint. Chill until needed.

Preheat the grill to medium. Season the lamb well and thread two or three cubes on to each skewer. Line the skewers up on lightly oiled baking sheets.

Grill for about six minutes, turning the skewers over halfway through. Serve on warm platters, with extra mint scattered over and the chutney alongside.

SWEET POTATO SAMOSAS

HANDS-ON TIME: 30 MINUTES

2 tbsp groundnut oil
2 tsp mustard seeds
3 tsp cumin seeds
1 onion, finely chopped
3 tsp finely grated fresh
   root ginger
2 garlic cloves, crushed
2 large sweet potatoes,
   peeled and diced into
   1cm cubes
2 green chillies, chopped
   (deseed if you like)
275g frozen peas, thawed
2 tsp garam masala
3 tbsp chopped coriander
juice of ½ lemon
2 x 270g packs or 12
   sheets of filo pastry
100g ghee or butter, melted

A simple raita of finely chopped cucumber, red onion and coriander or mint stirred into yogurt would be lovely on the side. Up the chillies, or use some that are ferociously strong, if you want hotter samosas. Makes 24.

Heat the oil in a large pan. Add the mustard seeds with 1 tsp of the cumin seeds. When the mustard seeds start to pop, add the onion, ginger and garlic and sauté for about five minutes. Throw in the sweet potato, chilli and 3 tbsp water and cook for another few minutes, stirring from time to time, until the potato is just tender.

Remove from the heat and stir in the peas, garam masala, coriander, lemon juice and salt to taste.

Preheat the oven to 190°C/fan 180°C/375°F/gas mark 5. Take one sheet of pastry at a time (keep the rest covered with a clean, damp tea towel to stop it drying out), cut into two strips and brush lightly with ghee or butter. Take one strip, lay it out on the work surface and place a heaped tablespoon of the filling at the end nearest you. Lift up the bottom left-hand corner of the strip and fold it diagonally over the filling. Continue folding diagonally to the end of the strip; you will have a triangular parcel. Brush with more ghee or butter and transfer to an oiled baking sheet. Repeat to make 12 parcels and brush lightly again with ghee or butter.

Sprinkle each samosa with the remaining cumin seeds and bake for about 15 minutes, until lightly browned.

STICKY TAMARIND CHICKEN WINGS

HANDS-ON TIME: 15 MINUTES

60g tamarind
2 tbsp groundnut oil
3 tbsp runny honey
3 tbsp dark muscovado
  sugar
2 tbsp soy sauce
thumb-sized piece of fresh
  root ginger, finely grated
2 fat garlic cloves, crushed
1 tsp dried chilli flakes
24 small chicken wings

In the realm of the sticky wing, sweet-sour, caramelised deliciousness reigns. Try these on the barbecue in summer. The glaze is also wonderful with pork and duck. If at all possible, try to get hold of a pliable block of tamarind, the kind with the flat seeds hidden among the dark brown pulp and accompanying fibre; you can buy it at Asian food shops and even some supermarkets. I just don't rate those acerbic little pots of tamarind puree; none of the subtlety of the tangy fruit remains.

Place the tamarind in a bowl and pour over 100ml boiling water. Mix with a fork and set aside for a few minutes. Strain through a coarse sieve, pressing the pulp down with the back of a spoon. Add the tamarind liquid to the oil, honey, sugar, soy, ginger, garlic and chilli in a large bowl and mix well. Add the wings, stirring to coat thoroughly, and set aside in a cool place for half an hour, or chill overnight if you can.

Preheat the oven to 200°C/fan 190°C/400°F/gas mark 6 and season the wings. Spread out on baking trays in a single layer and cook for about 25–30 minutes, turning once, until browned, lacquered and sticky. Serve hot, with napkins on hand.

RICE PUDDING SQUARES WITH STAR ANISE PLUMS

HANDS-ON TIME: 30 MINUTES

400g risotto rice
1.8 litres milk
400g caster sugar
1 large cinnamon stick
300ml double cream
4 large free-range eggs,
  beaten
2 free-range egg yolks
finely grated zest of
  1 orange
Star Anise Plums (see
  right)
cream, to serve (optional)

Rice pudding polarises mankind, so be prepared; you'll never win the battle with the most vehement haters. This recipe actually makes a dense cake that can be sliced neatly once chilled. A boon for portioning up at a party. Start this well in advance, a couple of days ahead if you can.

Start the day before, or even two days before. Measure the rice, milk and sugar into a very large saucepan and add the cinnamon stick and a pinch of salt. The mixture will be very sweet, but don't be concerned.

Bring to the boil very slowly, stirring occasionally, then reduce the heat and simmer gently, stirring often, for 20 minutes, until the rice is cooked and a lot of the liquid has been absorbed. It will thicken further on cooling. Stir in the cream and set aside to cool for at least two hours, stirring occasionally to prevent a skin forming. Chill overnight, if you have time, but it's better to use the night to chill the finished cake if you only have one to spare.

Meanwhile, line a 28x34cm baking tin with non-stick baking parchment and preheat the oven to 160°C/fan 150°C/325°F/gas mark 3. Add the eggs, yolks and zest to the rice and mix well, fishing out the cinnamon stick as you do so. Pour into the prepared tin, smooth out evenly and bake for about 40 minutes, until golden. The mixture will be a bit wobbly in the middle but that's a good thing. Set aside to cool for a good couple of hours and chill for a couple of hours more; overnight would be even better.

On the day, turn the cake out on to a board. Peel the paper away and cut into 24 even portions. Serve each piece in a small bowl, or on a saucer, with a Star Anise Plum half on top (see right), some of their syrup spooned over and a spoon on the side. Offer extra cream too, if you like.

To make **STAR ANISE PLUMS**, halve and stone 12 dark plums. Sprinkle the cut side of each half with a large pinch of sugar - I use demerara - and place a large frying pan over medium heat. Working in two batches, add half the plums to the pan, cut sides down. Cook for one to two minutes, until just beginning to caramelise. Remove to a plate and repeat with the remaining plums. Now add 400ml port or red wine to the pan with four star anise flowers, 200ml water and 250g demerara sugar. Bring to the boil and simmer briskly for 15 minutes, until syrupy. Tip in the plums and warm through for a minute, being careful as you want to preserve their shape. Remove from the heat, squeeze over the juice of half an orange and serve warm or cold. They'll actually be better, and the syrup more perfumed, if you can make them the day before. If plums aren't in season, the recipe will be just as delicious if you make a simple substitution. Dispense with the caramelising and gently poach 24 whole, stoned Agen prunes in the simmering star anise liquid for 10 minutes instead.

LIGHT AND STORMIES

HANDS-ON TIME: A COUPLE OF MINUTES

60ml light rum
about 120ml traditional
  ginger beer, to taste
ice and lime slices, to serve

The thought would probably make any soldier worth his salt drop his cocktail glass, but I prefer a light rum here; a very dark, spicy rum can jostle with the ginger a little too much. Make this with a proper, traditional ginger beer (something like Fentimans); glorified lemonade just won't cut it. These quantities will make two drinks.

Fill a couple of highball glasses with ice. Pour the rum and the ginger beer into each, using as much - or as little - ginger beer as you want. Serve the cocktails with a thin slice of lime on the side.

To make truly beautiful **ORANGE BLOSSOM MIMOSAS**, pour enough chilled, freshly squeezed orange juice into champagne flutes (or whatever glasses you've got handy) to fill them by a third. Add one or two drops of orange blossom water to each glass. (Drop it in from a teaspoon; you only need a tiny hint so as not to overpower the fizz.) Top up with chilled champagne and drink straight away.

LATE SPRING TEA PARTY FOR 12

Egg and Watercress Rolls

Garden Platter with Prawns and
Smoked Mayonnaise

Early Strawberry and
Elderflower Sponge

Macadamia Honeycomb
Ice Cream Cones

Lemon Verbena Lemonade

This is tea, not lunch, so it features rather a lot of sweet food. Unless you're The Queen, I imagine you don't hold tea parties every day, so it is intended as a bit of an old-fashioned treat. An afternoon for lashings of ginger beer and champagne and a dog called Timmy. As usual, practically everything can be made or prepared well in advance, ready to carry outside to a big table or picnic blanket in the garden. Eat the ice cream quickly, before it melts.

EGG AND WATERCRESS ROLLS

HANDS-ON TIME: 15 MINUTES

5 free-range eggs
25g soft butter, plus more
    for the rolls
2 tbsp milk
12 small, soft bread rolls,
    white or brown
watercress leaves, any
    coarse stalks removed

Sometimes the golden oldies can't be bettered. I've been making egg sandwiches like this for more than 20 years and, though I'm fickle enough to neglect them for months - even years - in between, whenever the need for an old-fashioned sandwich strikes, this is how I'd go about it:

Cover the eggs (make sure they're not too fresh or they'll be hard to shell) with cold water and bring to the boil. Once boiling, set the timer and simmer for five minutes.

Refresh briefly under cold water and peel. Put the warm eggs in a mixing bowl, add the butter and the milk and use a small knife to chop the eggs into small pieces. The residual heat will melt the butter. Season generously with salt and pepper and divide between the buttered rolls with a little watercress.

For every enthusiast falling upon an egg sandwich with glee, there will be an ardent hater. This is merely the way of the world. The naysayers might be interested in some **OTHER NATTY SANDWICH IDEAS,** so I've listed a few below to get you thinking. Use whichever bread you prefer but, in deference to the posh picnic, cut off the crusts and slice the filled sandwiches into triangles or fingers. Try these:

Soft goat's cheese, tapenade and basil ★ Finely sliced radish, cucumber and salted butter ★ Blue brie, wild rocket and ripe fig ★ Marinated artichoke hearts, fresh pesto and buffalo mozzarella ★ Roast beef slices, crème fraîche and horseradish ★ Prosciutto, tomato, avocado and mayonnaise ★ Sliced sausage, basil leaves and peperonata ★ Hot-smoked salmon and wasabi cream

Use a vegetable peeler to pare the zest from a couple of lemons in thick strips. Cut the lemons in half and squeeze out the juice. Add the juice and zest to a large saucepan with about 30 lemon verbena leaves, 500g caster sugar and a litre of water. Bring to the boil slowly, stirring to dissolve the sugar, and simmer gently for five minutes. Set aside to cool, then strain into sterilised bottles (see page 89) and keep in the refrigerator for up to a month.

To make **LEMON VERBENA LEMONADE**, pour a little of your lemon verbena cordial into tall glasses that you have first crammed with ice and lemon slices. Dilute with sparkling water to taste and add a shot of gin for those who give the nod.

GARDEN PLATTER WITH PRAWNS AND SMOKED MAYONNAISE

HANDS-ON TIME: 20 MINUTES

FOR THE MAYONNAISE

3 large, free-range
  egg yolks
a pinch of smoked sea salt
  (or normal sea salt)
1 tsp hot smoked paprika,
  to taste
150ml mild-flavoured
  olive oil
300ml groundnut oil
lemon juice, to taste

FOR THE REST

600g cooked, tail-on
  tiger prawns
300g baby fennel,
  trimmed and halved
  from top to bottom
300g baby carrots,
  scrubbed
200g pink radishes, with
  leaves, washed
2 heads Little Gem lettuce,
  leaves washed and
  separated
100g rustic Italian bread
  sticks
2 large, wide but shallow
  bowls, part-filled with ice
  cubes, to serve

The remains of Project Cold Smoker, last year's DIY debacle, slump reproachfully at the end of my roof terrace. And I had such grand plans for smoking magnificent sides of salmon, burnished kippers and pork bellies... For the sane, or the similarly DIY-challenged, sweet or sweet-hot paprika and smoked sea salt will donate a smoky flavour. You don't have to use the fancy salt, but I highly recommend seeking out good smoked paprika. This mayonnaise is particularly good slathered in an elegant smoked chicken and rocket sandwich.

It's easiest to make the mayonnaise in a food processor, but you can use a bowl, a whisk and a strong arm. Briefly blend or whisk the yolks with the salt and paprika. Start adding the olive oil with the blades (or whisk) running, drop by drop. As the oil is incorporated you may increase the flow to a thin trickle, but don't go too fast or it may split. Start adding the groundnut oil, gradually increasing the trickle until the mayonnaise is thick and shiny. If it splits, whisk another yolk into the mixture to bring it back and continue adding the oil. Brighten the seasoning with lemon juice and more paprika, if you want. Check the seasoning and whisk in a little warm water if it's too thick.

Pile the prawns into a couple of pint glasses or sturdy pots and stand in one of the ice cube bowls. Spoon the mayonnaise into three or four pots to stop people fighting over it - I use teacups - and nestle one beside the prawns. Stand the other pots of mayonnaise amongst the ice cubes in the remaining bowl, to keep it cool. Pile the vegetables prettily on a large plate, the lettuce on another and sit the bread sticks in a jar or tall glass alongside. All is ready.

EARLY STRAWBERRY AND ELDERFLOWER SPONGE

HANDS-ON TIME: 25 MINUTES

FOR THE CAKE
225g unsalted butter,
  very soft
225g caster sugar
4 free-range eggs,
  lightly beaten
250g self-raising flour
½ tsp baking powder
2 tbsp ground almonds
1 tbsp fresh or dried
  elderflower blossoms
  (optional)
4 tbsp milk
finely grated zest of
  1 lemon

**FOR THE ELDERFLOWER
  SYRUP**
120ml Elderflower Cordial
  (see page 183)
finely grated zest and juice
  of ½ lemon
1 tbsp demerara sugar

The fragrance of elderflowers is difficult to capture in a cake batter; their perfume becomes elusive after a stint in the oven. After much experimentation, the best way seems to be through including the fresh or dried blossoms in the mix, with a generous soaking in elderflower syrup afterwards for the warm sponge. Dried blossoms are available in some health food shops, but fresh would be preferable if you can gather your own. The recipe won't suffer much without either so don't run yourself ragged searching for them; elderflowers are only in season in early summer. If you have procured yourself some frothy, fresh blossoms, shake them well to dislodge any little bugs before decorating the cake.

Preheat the oven to 180°C/fan 170°C/350°F/ gas mark 4. Line the base and sides of a deep 23cm springform cake tin with non-stick baking parchment. Cream the butter and sugar together until light and fluffy. Gradually add the eggs as you continue to beat, adding a spoonful of flour to stabilise the mixture if it starts to curdle (though that doesn't matter too much). Sift over the flour and baking powder, add the ground almonds, elderflowers (if using), milk and zest and fold in with a large metal spoon or a spatula. Scrape into the tin, level the surface and bake in the middle of the oven for 40–45 minutes, until risen and golden brown. Loosely cover the cake with a layer of baking parchment or foil if it is browning too much.

Meanwhile, combine the elderflower cordial, lemon zest and juice and demerara in a small jug. The demerara is not dissolved, as it will provide a crunch on top of the cake.

Leave the cake to cool in the tin for five minutes, then use a skewer to puncture the warm sponge several times and pour the elderflower syrup over the top. Leave the cake to cool completely in the tin.

Hull a third of the strawberries and use a fork to crush with the caster sugar and 1 tbsp of the elderflower cordial. Pass the mixture through a sieve to remove the strawberry seeds. You can keep things rustic by just crushing the berries, sugar and cordial together with a fork, if preferred.

Just before serving, hull the remaining strawberries and halve any large ones. Put into a bowl. Whip the cream with the remaining 2 tbsp cordial, until it just holds a floppy shape. Marble the strawberry puree through the cream, being careful not to over-mix so you keep the rippled effect. Pile into a bowl and set beside the cake, ready to spoon on to each serving plate. Pile a few fresh elderflower heads on top of the cake, if you have them.

Serve each slice with the hulled strawberries and marbled strawberry cream.

FOR THE STRAWBERRY CREAM
600g early British strawberries
2 tbsp caster sugar
3 tbsp Elderflower Cordial (see page 183)
450ml double cream
fresh elderflower heads, to decorate (optional)

MACADAMIA HONEYCOMB
ICE CREAM CONES

HANDS-ON TIME: 40 MINUTES

FOR THE HONEYCOMB
2 tbsp white wine vinegar
200g golden syrup
300g caster sugar
1½ tsp bicarbonate of soda

FOR THE ICE CREAM
150g macadamia nuts
580ml tub double cream
400g can condensed milk

It must be the way the caramel foams scarily when you add the bicarb but any recipe for, or including, honeycomb or cinder toffee is pure alchemy and kids especially love helping to make it. Even if the dentist doesn't love them eating it. When stirred into this ridiculously easy ice cream base, honeycomb pieces all but turn to dreamy, liquid toffee, with just a hint of residual crunch at the centre. No special equipment is needed but, should you be the proud owner of an ice cream machine (and I'd wholeheartedly recommend buying one to anybody considering it), any plain or vanilla ice cream base, churned in a machine according to its instructions, will be lovely here. Just keep it on the less-sweet side because of all the honeycomb and nuts you'll be stirring in. As for the cones, though the brandy snap-like versions here are very simple and can be made a day in advance, they are there to gild the lily. Do use bought ice cream cones instead if you'd prefer.

Start with the honeycomb up to three days in advance. Line a large baking tray with non-stick baking parchment. Heat the vinegar, syrup and sugar together gently, until the sugar dissolves completely. Increase the heat and boil, without stirring, until the mixture turns the colour of dark amber. Remove from the heat and sift over the bicarbonate of soda. Quickly stir it in and pour the foaming mixture into the tin. Leave to cool and harden, then break or smash into small pieces.

Now for the ice cream: preheat the oven to 180°C/fan 170°C/350°F/gas mark 4 and spread the nuts out on a baking tray. Toast in the oven for six to eight minutes until pale golden, shaking halfway through. Set a kitchen timer or stay right by the oven, as macadamias are pricey and they burn frustratingly easily. Cool and chop roughly.

Whip the cream until soft peaks form, then add the condensed milk and whisk again until thick but not stiff. Reserve a couple of tablespoons of the chopped nuts and fold the rest into the cream mixture with two-thirds of the honeycomb. Scrape into a large, freezable container, cover and freeze for at least four hours, or preferably overnight. Keep the remaining honeycomb and nuts to serve.

To make the ice cream cones, form a couple of cone-shaped moulds out of double layers of foil and lightly butter the outside of each. Each should be about 13cm long and wide enough to hold a scoop of ice cream. Make sure the oven is set to 180°C/fan 170°C/350°F/gas mark 4 and line a large baking tray with non-stick baking parchment.

Gently heat the sugar, syrup and butter in a pan, until the sugar has dissolved. Remove from the heat and stir in the flour. Drop a tablespoon of this on to the lined baking tray to form a circle. Repeat to make two or three in total. Make sure each is spaced well apart as the mixture will spread as it heats up. Bake for approximately six minutes, until dark golden, then remove from the oven and leave to settle for half a minute. Lift up a warm circle with a spatula and quickly curl it around a cone mould with your hands, pinching the pointed end to seal. Leave to set for a minute, then carefully unmould and transfer to a wire rack. Repeat until all the mixture is used. If the baked circles cool too much to be pliable, return them to the oven for a minute to soften up. By the end, you should have at least 12 cones. Keep in an airtight container for up to a day.

To serve, carefully sit a scoop of ice cream in each cone and sprinkle with the reserved crushed honeycomb and macadamias. The trick is to finish the ice cream before it melts through the cones.

FOR THE CONES
100g unsalted butter, plus
  more for the moulds
100g light soft brown sugar
75g golden syrup
80g plain flour, sifted

GLAZED CARROT BIRTHDAY CAKE

SERVES 10-12
HANDS-ON TIME: 30 MINUTES

FOR THE CAKE
240g self-raising flour
1 tsp baking powder
1 tsp bicarbonate of soda
½ tsp salt
2 tsp ground cinnamon
1 tsp ground ginger
320g soft light brown sugar
250ml vegetable or very
  mild olive oil
4 free-range eggs
200g carrots, finely grated
100g pecan nuts or
  walnuts, chopped
4 balls stem ginger, finely
  chopped, plus 4 tbsp of
  the syrup

FOR THE FILLING
100g mascarpone
100g fromage frais
2 tbsp caster sugar

FOR THE GLAZE
120g caster sugar
100g mascarpone
½ tsp ground cinnamon
1 tbsp lemon juice
60g pecan nuts or walnuts,
  chopped fine

Carrot cake doesn't have to be worthy and brown sandal-wearing. A spiced, nutty sponge can rival the best of them in the indulgence stakes and this is a gorgeous, grown-up birthday cake. The caramel and mascarpone glaze is a fancy variation on cream cheese icing; it makes this suitable for dessert as well.

Line the bases and sides of two 23cm round cake tins with non-stick baking parchment. Preheat the oven to 180°C/fan 170°C/350°F/gas mark 4. Sift the dry ingredients, except the brown sugar, into a large bowl. In another bowl, beat the sugar, oil and eggs together and stir in the carrots, nuts, ginger and syrup. Pour this into the dry ingredients and mix. Divide between the tins and bake for 25 minutes, until risen and springy to the touch. Leave to cool for five minutes, then turn out to cool completely on a wire rack.

To make the filling, briefly beat the mascarpone, fromage frais and sugar together. Don't overbeat or the mascarpone can split. Or go runny. Mascarpone can be temperamental stuff if you don't treat it nicely.

Sit one cake on a serving plate and spread thickly with the filling. Sit the other cake on top. Gently heat the sugar and 3 tbsp water in a heavy-based saucepan, stirring until the sugar dissolves. Increase the heat and boil until the syrup turns to golden caramel. Remove from the heat and add 2 tbsp water; it will splutter. Use a wire whisk to stir in the mascarpone, cinnamon and lemon juice, until smooth. Leave to cool and thicken for a minute or so, then pour over the top cake, letting the glaze run down the sides in rivulets. Scatter with the nuts and stick in a few candles, if appropriate. And if candles are appropriate, you must sing.

HOT SUMMER BARBECUE FOR SIX

Skirt Steaks with Red Chimichurri
Sauce, Tortillas and Sour Cream

■

Charred Sweetcorn Salsa

■

Avocado Salsa

■

Best Brownies

As is usually the case, the barbecue will imbue
these recipes with a certain charred something
(apart from the brownies, that is, I'd recommend
bowing to a conventional oven for those), but they
can all be cooked with a grill or griddle instead. The
Argentine-style beef marinade is on the feisty side
of hot, so tone down the cayenne if you don't do so
well with chilli. It will keep in a chilled screw-top jar
for a few weeks, ready to put a rocket up chicken,
lamb, pork or prawns as a marinade, or grilled
vegetables as a sauce.

SKIRT STEAKS WITH RED CHIMICHURRI SAUCE, TORTILLAS AND SOUR CREAM

HANDS-ON TIME: 25 MINUTES

FOR THE MARINADE

100ml good sherry vinegar
3 tbsp extra-virgin olive oil
3 fat garlic cloves,
  finely chopped
2 fresh bay leaves, torn
1½ tsp cumin seeds,
  toasted and ground
1 tbsp hot paprika
½ tsp cayenne pepper
1 tsp coarsely ground
  black pepper

FOR THE STEAKS

6 x 200g skirt steaks
12 good-quality soft corn or
  flour tortillas
400ml sour cream, to serve
salad leaves, to serve

Bavette, a similar cut to skirt, taken from the the flank of the cow, is appreciated in France, where they know how to get the best from it, but these similar flank and skirt cuts aren't so widely loved in the UK. Traditionally, the butcher would take it home for himself, hence its other name of butcher's steak. It has enjoyed a bit of a revival of late, mostly because it's such good value. Look for the largest cut - goose skirt for this recipe - and ask your butcher to slice it with the grain into individual steaks. Always treat it carefully, either with long, slow braising to tenderise or, as here, with a punchy marinade and a high heat, for the juiciest barbecued steak.

Combine all the marinade ingredients and pour half into a non-metallic dish. Add the steaks and set aside to marinate for an hour. Reserve the remaining marinade (this is the chimichurri sauce). Meanwhile, get the barbecue good and hot. Wrap the tortillas thickly in foil and place on a not-so-hot area of the barbecue grill to warm through.

Lift the steaks from the marinade, season with salt and sear on a hot barbecue grill for about two minutes on each side, for rare, three on each side for medium-rare, or until done to your liking. (These are only guideline times as steaks will vary in thickness.) Most important is to remove the cooked steaks to a warmed plate and let them rest for five minutes before cutting.

Slice the rested steaks across the grain and accompany with the warm tortillas, sour cream, salad and the Salsas (see right). Serve the reserved chimichurri sauce alongside to spoon over the steak and salad.

CHARRED SWEETCORN SALSA

HANDS-ON TIME: 15 MINUTES

4 large corn cobs
2 green chillies, deseeded
  and finely chopped
400g can black beans,
  rinsed and drained
juice of ½ lime
1 tsp brown sugar
small handful coriander
  leaves, chopped

Dry-fried sweetcorn takes on a certain chewy nuttiness. It is quite delicious when paired with black beans and perked up with a touch of lime and coriander.

Using a small, sharp knife, cut the kernels from the sweetcorn cobs, running as close to the central cores as you can. Heat a large frying pan over a medium-high flame (or a sturdy pan on the barbecue grill) and add the corn with the chillies. Dry-fry for about 10 minutes, stirring often, until the kernels are browned. Set aside to cool.

Once cooled, add to the beans in a serving bowl with the lime juice, sugar, coriander leaves and a sprinkle of salt. Stir well and serve.

To make an **AVOCADO SALSA** with smoky depth, place a double sheet of foil on the grill of a barbecue and place four small plum tomatoes, one jalapeno or long red chilli and three unpeeled garlic cloves directly on it. You could also use a smoking hot griddle pan. Cook for about 10 minutes, turning with tongs every now and then, until the tomatoes are blackened and blistered all over and the chillies and garlic are soft. Set aside to cool. Halve and stone three large avocados and mash coarsely. Squeeze the juice of half a lime over and stir in half a very finely diced red onion. Remove the stalks and seeds from the chilli and peel the skins from the garlic and tomatoes. Crush the garlic and chilli in a pestle and mortar with a large pinch of sea salt. Add the peeled tomatoes, with any of their collected juices, and pound to a rough paste (or use a food processor to puree the garlic, chilli, salt and tomatoes coarsely). Mix into the avocado mixture with a small handful of chopped coriander leaves to finish.

BEST BROWNIES

HANDS-ON TIME: 20 MINUTES

300g dark (at least 70%
  cocoa solids) chocolate,
  broken into pieces
250g unsalted butter
4 large free-range eggs
200g caster sugar
150g light brown soft sugar
1 tsp vanilla extract
120g plain flour
½ tsp baking powder
½ tsp salt
20g cocoa powder

If you're dubious about the need for yet another brownie variant, may I take a moment to convince you? These squidgy little numbers have been honed to perfection over many years and I've never known anyone not ask for the recipe. As additions go, I'm not really a fan of nuts in my brownies, but don't let that stop you throwing in a handful of chopped walnuts or pecans. And the dark chocolate pieces can be changed to milk or white or all three; I have been known to double them to a generous 200g. This makes 16 bars or 32 smaller squares.

Line a 23x32cm brownie tin (or baking tin at least 5cm deep) with non-stick baking parchment. Preheat the oven to 190°C/fan 180°C/375°F/gas mark 5. Melt 200g of the chocolate with the butter: you can microwave them, but the highbrow way is to use a bowl set over simmering water. If you're feeling brave/lazy/rebellious, put them in a small saucepan over low heat and stir occasionally, until smooth. Set aside to cool. Chop the remaining chocolate.

Beat the eggs, sugars and vanilla together in an electric mixer (or use handheld beaters) at high speed for a couple of minutes, to give a lighter, more velvety texture. Sift in the flour, baking powder, salt and cocoa, then pour in the melted chocolate. Beat briefly to combine, then stir in the chopped chocolate. Scrape into the tin, reduce the oven temperature to 180°C/fan 170°C/350°F/gas mark 4 and bake for 35–40 minutes, until almost firm in the middle. When warm or cool (leave to firm up in the tin for at least 15 minutes before you start wielding that knife), turn out carefully and cut into 16 bars or 32 small squares. They'll keep in an airtight container for up to four days.

ELDERFLOWER CORDIAL

MAKES TWO 750ML BOTTLES
HANDS-ON TIME: 20 MINUTES

25 large, fresh elderflower
  blossom heads
2 lemons
1 small orange
2kg granulated sugar
75g citric acid

I guarantee you'll use this most beautiful of cordials often; it proves especially useful for non-drinkers at parties. Make up tall glassfuls with sparkling water, ice cubes and lemon slices, or slosh generously into creams, custards, ice creams and jellies to scent them with summer. You should be able to gather blossoms around May or early June. Citric acid is available at some chemists, or you can often find it in Asian food shops, tucked in among the spices.

Shake the elderflower blossoms to remove any bugs and extras. Do pick them from a rural hedgerow; dirty, roadside blooms will not be particularly appetising. Place the flower heads in a large bowl. Pare the zest from the citrus fruits using a vegetable peeler and thinly slice the fruits, pith and all. Add to the bowl.

Heat the sugar with 1 litre of water in a large pan until the sugar has dissolved. Bring gently to the boil, then remove from the heat, add the citric acid and pour into the bowl of blossoms and fruit. Cover with a saucepan lid and leave in a cool place for a day or two (no longer or the mixture may start to ferment).

Strain the cordial through a sieve, then through a layer of muslin. Divide between sterilised bottles (see page 89), seal and keep in a cool, dark cupboard for up to three months. Once opened, keep in the refrigerator until you have used it all up.

You don't have to plate food conventionally, especially at a **CASUAL PARTY**. Set up a table with a stack of bowls or plates and something beguiling to fill them. Warm, crusty bread rolls, plenty of Bramley apple sauce and a tray of herb-scented roast pork (not forgetting crackling) are easy for everyone to put together themselves and need nothing more than a salad on the side.

The same self-service treatment works wonders for a warm loaf of bread, a **REALLY BEAUTIFUL WHOLE CHEESE** - a round of Tunworth, perhaps - and a jar of fig jam. Set everything out on a wooden board with suitable knives and spoons. Asian salads of finely shredded vegetables and rice noodles won't wilt on standing and are substantial enough to hold their own.

SCALLOPS are self-portioning wonders, especially if you can serve them in their cleaned half-shells. A short cycle in a dishwasher is the easiest way to clean them. Whether you keep the corals on is up to you; I usually leave them attached. Simmer peeled and chopped parsnips in seasoned milk until tender then blend with butter, nutmeg and enough of the milk to make a purée. Keep this parsnip mixture warm. Fry some chunky cubes of pancetta in olive oil until browned and crisp then scoop out to drain on kitchen paper. Pat the scallops dry, season with salt, pepper and thyme leaves

and fry briefly in the pancetta fat, until crusty on the outside and tender within. Return the pancetta to the pan, just to warm through. Serve each seared scallop on the half-shell with a spoonful of parsnip purée, a cube or two of pancetta and a teaspoon on the side.

Learn to perfect a couple of **SIGNATURE COCKTAILS**. Start with the classics; they'll stand you in good stead and are a better bet than the latest fad. A beautifully made gin and tonic will be just the thing for most soirees. I like Hendricks, lime zest, large ice cubes and a proper, old-fashioned tonic water; Fever-Tree make a good example.

ICE LOLLIES are right up there with jelly and ice cream in the nostalgia stakes and don't take long to set. Wooden lolly sticks are dirt-cheap and silicone ice cube trays make brilliant moulds for a batch of lollies. Freeze highly flavoured (cold dulls sweetness) and unchurned granitas, sorbets, ice creams, fruit compotes and even cocktails (go easy on the booze, as too much alcohol will prevent the mixture freezing solid) in ice cube trays and stand a lolly stick in each while still a little slushy. The possibilities are endless: try pear and rosemary; blueberry yogurt; mojito; passion fruit and coconut; Vietnamese coffee...

I'm not generally a fan of tweaking recipes to the point where their character is lost, and have fond memories of scarfing down a more authentic version of these in Macau, but all-butter puff pastry and an easy custard make delectable **PORTUGUESE-STYLE CUSTARD TARTS**. To make 24 tarts, preheat the oven to 200°C/fan 190°C/400°F/gas mark 6. Roll up 300g rolled puff pastry to form a tight cylinder. Slice into 24 rounds; each should be about 1cm thick. Roll each out a little thinner, to line the holes of two lightly buttered 12-hole muffin tins. If they look a little raggedy, that's fine. Whisk five free-range egg yolks with a whole egg, 200g caster sugar and 4 level tbsp cornflour. Gradually whisk in 400ml single or double cream and 400ml milk. Pour into a pan and stir over medium heat until the mixture boils and thickens enough to coat the back of a spoon. Add the seeds from a vanilla pod, or a dusting of cinnamon, and cover the surface with clingfilm to prevent a skin forming. Divide the cooled custard between the pastry cases. Bake for 25 minutes, until browned. Cool in the tins for a few minutes, then transfer to wire racks to cool completely.

Warm 12 small bowls, ready to fill with a classic **EGG-FRIED RICE**. Stir-fry 400g raw prawns in groundnut oil in a wok until pink. Remove and add a couple of beaten free-range eggs, swirling until cooked.

Roughly chop the prawns and cut the omelette into strips. Increase the heat, add more oil and fry chopped garlic and ginger for a few seconds before stirring in 500g cold, cooked jasmine or basmati rice and heating through. Stir in the prawns and season with oyster sauce, soy sauce, sugar, salt and sesame oil. Fold in the egg with a handful of shredded spring onions and divide between the bowls. Stick a fork (this is not the time for chopsticks; there'll be rice all over the floor) into each and provide a bottle of chilli sauce.

Slowly fry a finely sliced onion until golden, then pep up with a sprinkle of cumin seeds, ground cinnamon, paprika and a few finely chopped dates. Remove from the heat and add 400g lean minced lamb, 3 tbsp breadcrumbs and a small beaten free-range egg. Scatter with chopped mint. Halve 12 sheets of filo pastry cross-wise and brush with melted butter. Fold in half and pile 1 heaped tbsp of lamb at one end, tuck in the edges and roll up to form a chubby cigar. Seal with beaten egg and brush with butter. Repeat to make 24. Bake for 20 minutes at 200°C/fan 190°C/400°F/gas mark 6, until golden. Stir 1 tbsp harissa into a small pot of Greek yogurt, sharpen with lemon and scoop into a bowl beside a pile of hot **LAMB CIGARS**.

Clondalkin Library
Monastery Road
Clondalkin
Dublin 22
Ph: 4593315

GLOSSARY

AFFOGATO Most conventionally vanilla ice cream, topped with a shot of strong, hot coffee and an optional shot of amaretto. Affogato (see page 21) literally means 'drowned' in Italian.

BRITISH Wherever possible, support our farmers and keep air miles down. Buy as local as you can.

BUTTER Use unsalted, partly for the flavour but mainly because it allows you to adjust the salt levels in recipes, especially sweet dishes, as needed.

CAKES When making cakes, prevent unfortunate curdling, seizing and lumping problems by bringing all the ingredients to room temperature first.

CAMPER VANS Myrtle (the Hurtle) is a rather natty, pale blue, 1972 bay window Devon and she starts every time. Just in case you were wondering. Highly recommended for camping, festivals, beach trips and the like. Don't expect to get there particularly fast though; it's all about the journey.

CURRY LEAVES Much-loved in Sri Lankan and south Indian recipes, these are used to fragrance curries and coconut milk. Fresh are most definitely preferable to dried. Find them at Asian food shops and some supermarkets and keep, wrapped in damp newspaper, in the refrigerator for a week.

DAIKON (OR MOOLI OR WHITE RADISH) Resembling a large, white, smooth parsnip, the daikon responds well to pickling (see page 110). The flesh is mild, crisp and surprisingly rich in vitamin C, and the skin is thin; peel it before using. It can easily be grated or shredded to be used in Asian and south-east Asian dishes.

EGGS All eggs in this book are medium, unless otherwise specified. Please, please buy free-range, organic if you wish. It's really not worth supporting the production of battery eggs for the sake of a few pennies. I particularly love Old Cotswold Legbar eggs for their stunning, sunset yolks.

Very fresh eggs are best for poaching (they will hold together well); slightly older eggs are best for boiling (they will be easier to peel because the egg will have pulled away from the shell slightly); more mature eggs are best for meringues, macarons and soufflés (the whites will break down to whip up beautifully and hold in the air).

FREE-RANGE MEAT If you are a meat and/or poultry eater, and you can possibly afford it, please buy free-range.

GALANGAL A member of the ginger family, galangal is a beautiful pale, rose-edged rhizome, commonly used in south-east Asian, east Asian and Indian cookery. Though it is tender when young, the roots we get here (buy it in Asian food shops) are often slightly tougher and more fibrous so will need peeling with a sharp knife and chopping or grating. It has a fresh perfume with a citrussy note. Add to curry pastes (see page 68) and marinades.

GELATINE The leaves are so much easier to use than powder or granules. Soak them in cold water for a few minutes to soften, then squeeze out and dissolve in hot (but not boiling) liquid. Never boil gelatine for standard mousse or jelly recipes, or it will lose its setting power. And bear in mind that liquid containing alcohol or lots of lemon juice will need extra gelatine to set it.

KAFFIR LIME The dark green, glossy leaves have an unrivalled and quite beautiful fragrance when infused in custards, sauces and curries. Only the zest of the knobbly kaffir lime itself comes anywhere close. The leaves and fruit can be difficult to buy fresh because of importing issues (they usually come from south-east Asia). Slice the leaves as finely as you possibly can, using a scalpel if at all possible. The easiest way is to roll a pile of the leaves up into a cigar shape and cut the sausage into fine slices. Discard the tough, stalky centre of each leaf.

KULFI A kulfi is a rich, frozen dessert, originally from India, made from reduced, sweetened milk (see page 105). It is very similar to ice cream and utterly delicious. Typically exotic flavours include mango, cardamom, saffron, rose and pistachio.

LEMON VERBENA A small shrubby plant with yellowy-green leaves that pack a really strong, lemony punch. It grows happily in Britain, and you should plant it, if you have room. Use the leaves to make teas and infusions, to scent custards and ice creams, in syrups (see page 171) for cordials and in marinades. If you can't find it, lemon zest and/or lemongrass will make an acceptable substitute.

NUOC MAM A Vietnamese fish sauce that has a categorisation system to rival that of olive oil. The best are light and sweet in flavour, not overly 'fishy', and should be used in dipping sauces (such as the confusingly named nuoc cham [see page 65] which is rich in lime); anything of lesser quality is best used in cooking. Look for the best sauces produced on the Vietnamese island of Phu Quoc.

PACHADI Vaguely translated as 'pounded' food, a pachadi from Kerala is typically yogurt-based (see page 116). It has much in common with raita, with a similarly refreshing purpose. Elsewhere in India, a pachadi can bear much closer resemblance to a chutney, with no yogurt in the mix.

POMEGRANATE MOLASSES When reduced right down in volume, pomegranate juice forms a magical, rust-brown or deep pink syrup, used in Persian cooking. Use it to add a sweet-sour tang to marinades, dressings and glazes.

RAS EL HANOUT Loosely transalated as 'top of the shop', this is the mix each Tunisian/Moroccan/Algerian spice vendor would blend from his best or favourite spices. Nutmeg, turmeric, ginger, cumin, coriander and cardamom tend to be mainstays, but other additions vary from the spicy (cayenne) to the romantic (dried rose petals). Use it as a rub for meat, poultry and fish, or add to marinades. Or use it to spice vegetables before roasting, or add to soups and stews.

SABAYON Sabayon in French; zabaglione in Italian. Either way, it is a deliciously frothy confection of sweet dessert wine, egg yolks and sugar (see page 105). Cream or mascarpone are sometimes added.

SEASONING Use beautiful salt and good, freshly crushed black pepper and use them well.

SMOKED SEA SALT Sea salt flakes take up the smoky flavour of wood chips very successfully. Use wherever you want to highlight delicate flavours (eggs, fish, simple vegetables [see page 173]), or whenever you want to show off. Find it in posh delis and bigger supermarkets.

SOBA NOODLES Made from resolutely nutty buckwheat, Japanese soba noodles make themselves incredibly useful in the kitchen, especially when time is short. They cook in no time, ready to be thrown into soups and salads.

SUGAR All 'white' sugar used in this book - caster, granulated, icing and the like - is of the unrefined or golden variety, unless otherwise specified. This is both for the subtle caramel flavour it gives and the buff tint. But, if pure white is all you have in the cupboard, then pure white is what you should use.

SYLLABUB An old English dessert with a most charming name. It most commonly contains wine and sweetened cream, whipped until frothy, light and softly mousse-like.

TAHINI Light tahini paste is the variety you'll want in the vast majority of cases, as it is less bitter than the dark. Milled from white sesame seeds (usually hulled), tahini is rich and dense and essential in all sorts of Middle Eastern recipes and beyond (China, Japan and Korea are also fond of sesame paste). It is particularly useful, I find, when cooking vegetarian food. And, of course, in houmous (see page 52). Find it in health food shops, delis, Middle Eastern food shops and larger supermarkets. Keep it in a cool place and give it a good stir before using, as the oils tend to separate in the jar.

THAI GLUTINOUS RICE Or sticky rice or sweet rice. Short-grained, starchy and delicious with coconut milk (see page 36), the white versions have been milled but some unmilled varieties may be a completely ravishing black or purple colour (see page 62). Give glutinous rice a good soaking in cold water - for up to 12 hours, if you can - before draining and rinsing well. This will both soften the grains and help them keep their identity once cooked.

WHEATGERM If you want to add extra nutrients - vitamin E, zinc, magnesium, folate, essential fatty acids - to cereals and baking, the easiest way is to throw in a little wheatgerm. It has a pleasing nutty flavour and is officially Good For You. Keep it chilled in a sealed bag to stop it picking up other flavours and/or turning rancid.

ZESTING Do buy one of those little, handheld zesters to zest lemons, limes and oranges and their ilk (and always buy unwaxed lemons if you are to use their zest). Attempting to use the zester part of a box grater is futile and will drive you slowly mad. You can never get the darned stuff out. Otherwise, use a small grater and stop before you reach the bitter white pith.

ACKNOWLEDGEMENTS

So many.

Claire, you've done such a marvellous job. Lucy, the most charming and patient editor there ever was. Anne, Helen and rest of the Quadrille team; you've made it all such a joy.

Ruth for capturing Myrtle and the Downs so perfectly and Myles-of-the-Darkness for all your help.

Elly and Heather, for the loveliest emails and for making it all happen.

Dearest Georgina, you're a joy and a wonder and we've laughed so much (just promise not to set off my giggles again just before/part-way through service). To Tom and Nick and all who so kindly helped and came along to The Hart & Fuggle. There'll be second helpings.

Dear Honey and Gug and Ian.

To William (top waiter extraordinaire) and all at WFI, especially Amber for being the best customer by a country mile and Katy for the blogging.

Yuki, Fliss, Tom, Tonia, Annabel, Rosie, Ben, Alex, Joey, Claire, Chris, Harriet and so many more. Here's to more time for supper in the future.

Almost lastly but never leastly, Tiggers love Emmas and Tabs madly, especially when you put them in a Forest House and add an Uncle Dan (who barely flinched at Myrtle-with-no-reverse-lights) and a pair, no less, of beautiful babies. Days with you can never be matched and are always too short; thank you so much.

And Mum and Dad, for your unfailing love and support.